Love is Demonstrated

Making Marriage
Sacred Again

Cover Design by
bespokebookcovers.com

Love is Demonstrated

Making Marriage
Sacred Again

Del Hall and Del Hall IV

Acknowledgments

It is with the deepest love and gratitude we thank the four married couples who shared the lessons and growth of their marriage. Their willingness to share some very personal and sacred marriage experiences and personal histories made this book a possible prototype for other marriages. These testimonies show that so much more is possible in your marriage when each partner puts God first. We hope that by reading these true stories you will be inspired to learn how to better demonstrate love in your marriage and in your relationship with God.

The authors would also like to thank all those who helped in the editing of this book: Brian Boucher, Joan Clickner, Lorraine Fortier, and David Hughes. Your keen eyes and thoughtful suggestions made a huge difference in the telling of these heartwarming stories.

"The days of any religion or path coming between me and my children are coming to an end" saith the Lord

December 29, 2013

Table of Contents

7. Sacred Union

8. Sacred Union

Appendix

Foreword

Our gratitude goes out to God and to Del and Lynne Hall, whose demonstration of putting God first in every area of their lives and of having a loving marriage inspired us to reach beyond the limitations of our past, to press on through challenges, and to more fully accept the blessings of God in our lives. We both feel that our message is one of hope and help. There are both in abundance, ready for you too at the perfect place and time.

Prophet blessed us with help, guidance, and healings. He also guided us through a series of opportunities to a place where we both surrendered all on the Altar of God. We both made a conscious choice to put God first. This was an incredible turning point in our marriage.

Once the conditions in our hearts were right we were able to accept and utilize the tools that God gave us to co-create a beautiful and abundant marriage. We did not just hear the advice, we did something with it. Accepting the Love of God means more than hearing good advice. It means accepting help beyond what we could have imagined and doing our part. The tools we were given were blessed by the Divine. Issues and pains of the past were healed that we could not heal ourselves.

The healing in our hearts and our marriage ended a cycle of divorce, hurt, and disrespect that went back many generations. Breaking this cycle has freed us, our children, and our future grandchildren from the bonds of this vicious pattern. The golden ripples will impact generations. For this and the Love of God, we are truly grateful.

Written by Chris and Molly Comfort

Preface

As I reviewed these beautiful stories of love I found myself relating to many of the challenges these couples faced. I am blessed with a beautiful and loving marriage, but as I read I saw areas where I could better demonstrate my love and respect for my wife. One moment I was laughing and the next moment crying. I was intrigued by the level of honesty and openness being shared and did not want to stop reading.

The four marriages in this book are all different, as are the eight individuals. Though these stories are not exactly your own story, they all have elements most any couple can relate to in their own marriage. Even couples not yet married can greatly benefit. I believe the lessons learned by these diverse couples could help future couples start their marriages off better than those in this book.

So what is the focus and pearl of this book? Each couple truly loves their spouse. All had difficulty in consistently DEMONSTRATING their love and respect in both words and actions. Love needs to be demonstrated to be of value. That seems to have been an issue within all four marriages. Also, each individual brought to the marriage old attitudes and habits. They all had developed expectations and brought these expectations into their relationship. Some had former marriages or relationships. All had examples of marriages from their parents, some which might be considered dysfunctional.

Each individual also had old scars and hurts, like we ALL do. Each had what I call negative passions of the mind, again, like we ALL do. These include anger issues, fear, vanity, unworthiness, lusts, and excessive attachments. When these strong negative passions of the mind are thrown into the marriage, hang on! This is where having help and guidance from a living Prophet of God can be life-saving. As a Prophet one of the first areas I help my students with is understanding the root of these passions and then reducing the control the passions have over their lives. Before going to the higher worlds one needs help with these strong negative passions. Reducing them not only helps one grow spiritually, but improves and balances daily life.

As a Prophet of God one of the opportunities I have is also helping couples learn to express and demonstrate the love they have for each other. For over thirty years I have led spiritual retreats in the mountains of Virginia. During these retreats we witness how God's Love and Grace can bless us in ways beyond what many know, believe, or have been taught is possible. Seemingly hopeless relationships can be renewed by the Divine Spiritual Keys and blessings I share at retreats. Couples who still have a spark of love for each other can uplift and renew their marriages to once dreamed of heights.

All eight of the testimonies in this book were written by students at the Guidance for a Better Life retreat center.

Prophet Del Hall III

Introduction

This book leads the reader through four marriages – eight unique stories. Anyone who has been in a relationship will be able to relate to these honest and heartfelt stories. What do they all have in common? They all celebrate how accepting help from the Divine can transform a marriage for the better. They show how when both partners have a trusting relationship with God obstacles to joy, peace, and love within a marriage can be overcome. All eight stories provide hope and point the way to a happier and more fulfilling marriage. Even if you are already blessed with a wonderful marriage it can always be better. This does not mean there will not be ups and downs and bumps in the road. It does mean you will have more strength, wisdom, guidance, and support to get through the tough patches quicker and with less wear and tear.

These stories also highlight the blessing of having a living spiritual guide, someone who can teach you how to better recognize and implement Divine guidance into your life. This guidance, which is ultimately a gift of love from

God, covers all areas of your life, including marriage. All the couples in this book have been blessed with a personal and loving relationship with God through the example and teachings of my father, Prophet Del Hall III. Mankind is never without a Prophet. We are never alone. This is the greatest proof of God's Love for man – a continuous unbroken chain of divinely chosen and trained Prophets sent to help show us our way home to the Heart of God and how to live a more abundant and love-filled life, including in our marriages.

As the authors grew in their ability to accept more of God's Love, it helped them to give and receive more love with their spouses. As they learned more about giving and receiving love with their spouse, it helped them in giving and receiving God's Love. The two relationships work hand in hand. One of the biggest obstacles many couples face is actually expressing their love for each other and doing so in ways their spouse can accept. It is not enough to simply love your spouse for a marriage to flourish – your love must be demonstrated and received for it to be of actual value. When your love is expressed, and ultimately received, a marriage can be transformed for the better. The Divine can help you find creative ways to express your love. If the

2

love is there, there is a way to make a more loving marriage a reality. Never give up on love!

All the authors know they are Soul, and Soul has the ability to receive loving guidance from the Divine in all areas of life – marriage most certainly included. Many are taught they "have" a Soul, but this is not true. The authors know they ARE Soul that has a physical body. They each know they are eternal spiritual beings within a temporal physical embodiment. When their physical body comes to its end, their real eternal selves, SOUL, will continue on. This seemingly simple change of perspective is actually of monumental significance. Soul has access to creativity, knows truth, and has a direct line of communication to receive loving guidance from the Divine. It is with Soul that God communicates through insights, dreams, intuitions, and knowingness. In this way the authors of these stories received Divine guidance that ultimately brought them more joy, comfort, and peace into their marriages.

The authors learned to not focus all of their time and effort on fixing a struggling marriage. Instead they made time to focus on their relationship with God and His chosen Prophet. They each in their own way made the following quote, "Seek ye first the Kingdom of Heaven and all these things will be added unto you" a reality.

It is with humility, reverence, and love that these authors share their very personal experiences, blessings, and insights about their marriages. Reading these true stories of everyday folks transforming their marriages through Divine love, guidance, grace and their own personal effort, may inspire you to do the same. They know you too can experience even greater joy and abundance in your marriage by opening yourself to the truth within these pages – a truth that has the power to set you free.

Del Hall IV

Note to the Reader

All the authors who contributed to this book sing HU daily in spiritual contemplation. They tune in and raise up spiritually by singing HU, which makes them more receptive to the guidance and Love of God and to God's Prophet of our times. A basic understanding of both the Prophet and HU will help you more fully understand the "Language of the Divine" shared in this book. Please refer to the Appendix for an introductory understanding of God's historical line of Prophets and the role they serve.

HU is a name for God, and when sung it becomes a love song to God. It is not really a word, it is a sound vibration. It has been around literally forever, way before the English language was created, or any Earthly language. It is pronounced like the word hue.

When we sing HU we become more receptive in allowing the Divine to help purify the lower self and the negative passions. The lower self, the physical mind and body, need help with the passions of the mind. These passions include anger, fear, greed, vanity, excessive attachments, worry, etc. Singing HU brings the potential to experience God's Light and Sound, which also purify. HU can bring clarity, strength, healings, health, and protection. The Divine determines the gift to be received, although we can ask for specific help, guidance, or clarity.

Singing HU UPLIFTS our consciousness, which enables us to experience a higher view of life. From a higher view we may more fully recognize truth. The truth might be about us, about the Divine, about a situation we are involved in, or clarity about someone else. From a higher view we have the opportunity to make better decisions. HU ALSO OPENS US to be more receptive of truth and other spiritual help being offered.

When we sing HU it brings spiritual nourishment to us, especially to our real selves, Soul. If we sing it every day it brings us our "daily spiritual bread." This builds spiritual stamina, like going to a physical gym daily to build physical strength. Soul needs nourishment just as our physical body needs food.

HU can be sung out loud or silently. When singing HU we are sending love and gratitude to God. God hears and recognizes our every HU, so we focus on each individual HU we sing. The quality of our voice is not as important as our intent to send love and gratitude.

It is good to set a few minutes aside daily for our relationship with God. One way to do so is by singing HU. It shows God that you want to draw closer to Him. The Divine will respond either during the HU, shortly after the HU, in a dream, in an awake dream, or in some other way whether we recognize the response or not.

When we are fearful, upset, or in grief, sing HU out loud or silently. Doing so often brings peace. When we experience peace we can hear Divine guidance more clearly. If in trouble sing HU and it may bring clarity of the situation. When we see a situation clearly we can make better decisions.

Singing HU is a pure prayer. It is not telling God what to do, but sending Him love. The love we send comes back to us in some form or fashion. The extra love we send to God goes to other Souls we may know and to Souls we may never meet. So singing HU not only blesses us but blesses others.

After singing HU for a few minutes or up to fifteen or twenty minutes, we sit still and quiet for a while and just listen with our heart. Over time and with practice we will recognize the Divine response.

Prophet Del Hall III

1

Never Give Up on Love
Chris' Story

"Don't ever give up on love." Prophet Del Hall III

Grenades and Landmines

My wife cussed at me.

My wife rarely ever said a bad word. It was simply not in her nature. It had taken me hours to wear her down emotionally for this to happen. Yet despite her obvious anger and hurt, I considered it a small victory in a verbal war that had been escalating for several hours. I could not say the same about my cussing, and I littered the verbal grenades I had been tossing at her with plenty of them. It added a little extra bang when they exploded. I could not at this moment remember exactly what had started the fight or what point I was even trying to make, but her cussing clearly meant a marked change in the momentum of the battle. I had somehow managed to get through her defenses. This was no small achievement. I had weathered icy walls of silence and a minefield of contempt to get here. At this point I was confident that in another forty-five minutes or so she was sure to concede, finally seeing the wisdom of whatever point I was trying to make. Peace would finally return between us, my beautiful wife would open her heart back up to me, and all would be well again...only that is not what happened after we fought. That was hardly ever what happened.

Still, I pursued my Pyrrhic victory with take-no-prisoners abandon as if I was being deprived of oxygen without it. In the process I ignored the ever-deepening hole I was going the extra mile to dig; the hole I felt like we would never get out of, and the only direction I ever seemed to be able to manage was deeper down into it.

My marriage produced three beautiful children in a wonderful home surrounded by family, friends, and loved ones, but issues between my wife and me always seemed to get in the way of any real stability. It was a relationship that for all practical purposes had been built on sand.

We had met at the Guidance for a Better Life retreat center in the beautiful Blue Ridge Mountains of central Virginia. We were both students there. It was (and remains) our favorite place on Earth. As students of Del Hall, the God-ordained Prophet of our times, we had each grown individually in our relationship with God and His chosen Prophet in the years we had been coming to retreat center.

When Molly and I began dating I knew immediately she was "the one." I never doubted she was a gift from God. If I was a gift to her however, she did not seem to have gotten that memo. I was not even on her radar, initially. It bruised my ego that my gift from God did not respond like one right away. I felt I was ready to love her for the rest of this life.

I did not realize however, that there was a test. I naively thought I could just walk in, proclaim my love, and sail away together into the sunset. I would love to reminisce about how calm I stayed during these trying times. How my resolve to love her never waivered. How stoic I remained in the face of adversity, but this was not the case. What began as "set in stone" confidence soon looked like a fleeting chance at best. I felt if I did not keep pressing on I was going to lose the love of my life.

At some point I gave away my peace. This is never a good trade-off, and it was disastrous here. Fear, anger, and neediness soon filled the void my missing peace left. My vision and my decisions became more and more shortsighted. Molly no longer had to push me away. I was doing the pushing for her, all the while shouting how much I loved her.

Molly and I were both children of divorce. None of that excused the weird, dysfunctional courtship we engaged in, but it probably explained a bit of it. As a young child I had listened to my own parents' icy silences erupt into arguing and yelling well into the early hours of the morning on many occasions. Healthy communication was just not part of my parents' skillsets. Somewhere that must have imprinted on me that arguing and yelling was usual in a marriage, a normal response to any disagreement. I have come to learn that disagreements are to be expected. They should not be looked at as threats to a relationship. They are a regular part of life and every healthy adult should have at least a few tools to handle them effectively without pushing their relationship toward Defcon Five. Yet well into my marriage the threat of disagreements was still lurking behind my wife's frequent silences and across her emotional minefield. I took up the challenge to try to defuse them.

Another of our challenges was cultural. I grew up in an environment where a friendly family discussion had a baseline volume that some would consider "yelling." Italians can be a loud, passionate people. To this day my wife and I disagree as to what is yelling and what is a conversational tone. I often approached disagreement itself as a volume issue. If someone, my wife in particular, disagreed with me, it meant they could not hear me. So I said it again. Louder. If they still did not agree, I graciously repeated myself until they were able to finally hear me. This rarely was an effective form of communication.

Still, it was no accident I incarnated with the parents I did. God put me in the best situation to grow spiritually in this lifetime. To me, parents can be a mirror of some of our strongest qualities, qualities we need to face in ourselves. The very issues I grew up resenting in my parents were helpful reference points when I was ready to face them in myself as an adult.

Now I am grateful for those experiences. They have helped mold me into who I am today, but as a child, the constant instability confused me. I can remember my father leaving unexpectedly abandoning my family. My grandfather called to tell me I was now the man of the house. I felt the weight of responsibility in his words. I had no idea what they meant at the time, and it did not occur to me to ask. I don't remember my father saying goodbye, but I do remember my uncertainty and the likelihood that he was not coming back.

I brought my lack of stability and abandonment issues into my relationship with Molly. It was certainly bumpy during the dating process, but if nothing else my persistence eventually paid off. Molly and I were married and blessed with three amazing children in five short years. Children soon occupied most of our time and often masked the lingering issues that festered under the surface. When things were good, they were wonderful, a glimmer of the potential I knew was there. Yet anger, distrust, and animosity grew alarmingly each year. We both knew each of our children was a gift from God, but as time marched on, Molly still did not seem to be feeling that way about me, and I was questioning when my gift was going to stop trying to blow me up as I scaled the outer defenses of her heart. By the time our youngest child was born, I had long stopped treating

Molly as a gift from the Divine that she was, and is.

So despite the blessings and abundance in our lives, we were closer to getting a divorce than reaching our tenth anniversary. The cliché of "the love is there, *but...*" very much fit our marriage then. The *but*, of course, meant the love was not being *demonstrated*. A wall of words, often harsh, bitter, and angry expressed our growing frustration and unhappiness. There seemed to be no way over, around, or through it. Even though it was painful, God was using the situation to help me face the hurt in my own heart - my insecurities, fears, and the urge to run permanently in the opposite direction.

A Daughter's Prayer

My daughter drew a picture when she was five years old. It is a drawing of two stick figures, one labeled *Mom*, the other *Dad*. They are holding hands, the mom smiling an enormous smile. The dad has two eyes but no expression whatsoever, not even a mouth. Under the two figures my daughter wrote (and adorably misspelled) the word *wedding*. It is one of the most beautiful drawings I have ever seen, not because it is technically beautiful, but because it is unabashedly hopeful and unreservedly loving – just like she is. At the time she drew it however, I did not embrace it, dismissing it as unrealistic and even a cruel reminder of the sad, painful state of my marriage. It triggered festering wounds and the certainty that I would never celebrate my marriage the way the mom and dad did in her drawing.

I now know her drawing was nothing less than a prayer. Despite much evidence to the contrary my daughter boldly and courageously expressed the prayer in her heart – to see her parents happily married, but our legacy as parents was looking more and more like we would pass the dysfunction and hurt on to not only them but their children as well. That weighed heavily on Molly and me.

Through the years, Molly and I had made many attempts to change course. We sat down to list what was missing in our relationship. We would select several things in areas we could do something about and set about to focus on those things instead of the negatives, but the change only went so far. Outer happiness cannot fix inner *un*happiness.

Part of the problem was karmatic in nature. Our first date, an unseasonably warm day in

March of 2005, was at a local historical attraction. During the tour I came across an old painting. Prophet blessed me with the immediate insight that I was connected to this scene over two hundred years ago. Before our date was over, I knew I had spent time at this place in a past life. Eventually we were able to connect the dots and recognize we had been married to each other in that lifetime. There were children then too. There were also many unresolved issues that followed us into this life. In fact, as we learned more about that lifetime, we saw how these issues had sprung up in an almost identical fashion in the present. There were issues of attachments to extended family members, emotional withdrawal, and separation. To a greater or lesser degree, all of these remained unresolved in the present, but God knows what is really in our hearts, and He will never give up on us.

Never Give Up on Love

There is a prayer by a Chinese Prophet of old which prays for the least and lowliest of God's servants to be led home to Him. Incredibly, that prayer has manifested for me. I am not a spiritual giant of old, just an ordinary person and yet, I am being led by Prophet back home to the very Heart of God. Prayer is powerful indeed. Sometimes the answer is no. And sometimes prayers are answered above and beyond what we could ever dream.

It was just before Christmas 2011. I was at an overnight retreat at Guidance for a Better Life. These winter retreats are smaller than classes held during the rest of the year. About twelve of us were sitting down for dinner in good spirits with Del and his wife Lynne. News that Prophet Del's son was soon returning home after a brief hospital stay was in the back of our minds. When I first heard the news, I was overjoyed. I immediately thought, "Prayer answered!" I know I was one of many praying for him.

When I heard he would be leaving the hospital I thought, "Wouldn't it be great if he was able to come home for Christmas?" That would be a real gift for his family. Then when I heard he would be coming home even sooner I thought, "Wouldn't it be great if we heard him drive by during the retreat?" But for him to arrive during dinner, and for me to be able to see my dear friend in person, was more than I could have hoped for. There was so much gratitude as he came through the door; it poured through the moment. Witnessing that was more than enough. I was grateful just to see him, but the Divine entrusted me and the others present with a moment I will not soon forget.

Del IV approached his dad and hugged him. He quietly expressed his gratitude and thanks. The prayer was answered. There in front of me were a father and son, grateful to see each other. It was a touching moment. We witnessed the loyalty, the devotion, and the demonstration of love they had, and have, for each other. It was moving beyond words. Del IV held his father's face in his hands and kissed his cheek. Then he said goodbye to the rest of us in the class and departed for his home.

If that moment was not blessing enough, Del sat back down at the dinner table, hardly having had time to process what just occurred. He turned and said to me, almost as an aside, "Don't ever give up on love." That moment and those words are written in my heart. As precious as that moment with his son might have been to him personally, he took a moment with me, one of the least of Thy servants. Ever the teacher, he simply saw the opportunity to teach and took it.

"Don't ever give up on love."

A Year of Healing and Grace

What does it mean to never give up on love? The words stirred me. There was more to them than generic fortune-cookie wisdom, but how specifically did the words apply to me? Not giving up on my spiritual path immediately resonated with me. Not giving up on the prayers of my heart did as well. Yes, Prophet could (and did) bring me to the very Heart of God, but righting my sinking marriage? That seemed out of the realm of possibility. In fact, it never occurred to me at the time those words could apply to my marriage.

Several years later in early 2014, the outcome for my marriage remained bleak. A few months before, Del had suggested I seek counseling. Counseling turned out to be even more of a blessing than I could have thought possible. I was diagnosed with dysthymia, a mild form of depression. It gave a name to the negative coping mechanism I used to deal with the strife I experienced in my marriage and life. The therapy was so successful; it added several new tools to help me be aware of my downward spirals. It was a relief to face the self-defeating fog I had been under. It was also a good example of God not removing an obstacle but rather giving me the tools to overcome it. This was a strong step to God changing my heart, but I had further to go before my marriage and life would bear the fruit of God's Grace.

Over the years, Molly and I had listened to marriage tapes and read books on having a more Godly marriage. Following Prophet's guidance, we implemented some of the suggestions we were led to, but we never gained enough momentum to break our downward spiral. We never could seem to clean the slate of the issues that plagued us from the past in order to focus on anything good there – at least not for very long. We went around and around in circles, spinning our wheels. We were both worn out. It was affecting every area of our lives. A big part of this dream life was dying, and I felt helpless to do anything about it.

Still, we are never abandoned by God and we are always in the Divine presence of His chosen Prophet. 2014 began a year of intense personal healing for me. Prophet's suggestion to seek therapy was only the tip of the iceberg. I am aware of at least four spiritual healings I received during the year. In addition, there was a physical healing that started a crack in the walls separating my wife and me.

At a May retreat at Guidance for a Better Life I received a major healing, one which in some ways paved the way for the amazing transformations that followed. A loving relationship with God and His Prophet is the most secure thing I can think of. It brings stability in a world of change and uncertainty. Yet my biological father's sporadic physical and emotional absences in my childhood had imprinted a fear of abandonment that affected my ability to give and receive love in all areas of my life. The insidious thing about fear of abandonment is that it makes you wary of the other shoe you are always expecting to drop. This was a huge obstacle to peace in my marriage and long-term success on the spiritual path.

One morning before class that May I walked down to a gorgeous clearing and sat on a stump, listening to the birds welcoming the morning with song. This was my quality time with the inner Prophet. With my heart open I enjoyed a silent contemplation. In this moment of tranquility came a sudden burst of emotion. I was suddenly crying and begging not to be left behind. My spiritual syllabus for that moment was to deal with the nagging wound of abandonment. Soon the intensity subsided and I sat soothed by Prophet's calming inner presence. I came out of the contemplation healed, to a large degree, of my abandonment issues. When I stood, I had a confidence that although every physical relationship would end Prophet would never abandon me. I practically bounced up the hill. I felt like an individual reborn to a future whose growth and splendor was now practically unlimited.

I received another healing during a June retreat that year. While I was talking in class with Prophet physically, I felt his hand spiritually reach into my heart and remove clumps of doubt and insecurities festering there. These were accumulated from this and past lifetimes. It was a handicap I carried, it seemed, for ages. Along with the old abandonment issues, this healing continued the cleansing of my heart with God's Grace. Later Prophet revealed an insight that the healing had helped me with a lifelong struggle in expressing myself (unfortunately being loud does not make up for ineffective communication). This block affecting me from my early childhood was gone.

Later that summer I had minor surgery. Though this was a physical healing, it had an unexpected impact on my relationship with Molly. For the operation to even occur required so many things to line up perfectly. It was a window of opportunity created by the Holy Spirit where my work schedule, sick time, and even my insurance coverage fell into place exactly when I needed it. The procedure was over in a few hours, and shortly I was home recovering in bed for what turned out to be two weeks. This gave me the opportunity to really depend more on my wife. My heart had hardened towards her during our marriage. Now, softened by pain and medication, I was able to let my guard down and truly accept her love and help more than I had in years. Though she had her own struggles with accepting love, Molly still had a simple need for me to accept *her* love. When I did not fight, resist, or reject it, I fulfilled a deep need in her. It alone was not enough to change the course in our marriage, but there were now definite and palpable cracks in the ice. Prophet had taken a seemingly disconnected event and woven it into the puzzle of our marriage, using it to soften each of us towards the other.

A Gift Class

Because we each had glimpsed a little bit of daylight through the cracks, both Molly and I had gotten our hopes up. A wave of disappointment brought us quickly back to reality like a late April snowstorm, yet God's timing is always perfect. Our marriage was no worse than it ever had been. In fact, it might have been a little better, but my tolerance for just getting by, for settling, and for "the love is there, *but...*" was gone. In her disappointment, my wife had left me emotionally. My beloved was all but lost, and I felt too worn out to do much about it.

In a place of resignation, I arrived at Guidance for a Better Life in November of 2014 for a weekend retreat. Every healing I had received throughout the year had brought me to this point, yet my heart remained heavy. I was out of ideas, patience, and motivation. I could no longer just survive in my marriage. My unhappiness with the state of my marriage, my life, and myself was slowly eating away at me inside. Something had to change.

Every retreat I have ever been to at Guidance for a Better Life has been a gift. This one especially so. All the healings and Grace that had been showered over me throughout the year had laid an incredible foundation. I had gained confidence and clarity and a great deal of security, but the pieces of the puzzle had to be put together for the full transformation to take place.

From the time I stepped onto the property I began to relax. In my experience, it is much harder to hear Spirit when we are uptight. We keep asking, we keep praying with more volume and intensity, and wonder why God does not answer us. Sometimes, stepping back to take a deep breath and actually listen, with our ears *and* our heart, makes all the difference. This is almost impossible without a measure of peace in our hearts.

There is a plus factor being in the physical presence of a true Prophet of God. Though communication extends beyond the physical, being there in person has its benefits. The help does not have to stop when we leave the property, but sometimes we need to be in the *presence* to be healed of what is ailing us spiritually. Within an hour of being on the property, I was given an inner insight by Prophet to a simple exercise to try when I went home. It was brilliant in its simplicity. No words were spoken outwardly, but Prophet, adept at reading and speaking to hearts, spoke directly to mine.

I was energized by the clarity of the communication. In my experience, those who hear the whisperings of Spirit most accurately accept God's blessings. They have more abundant lives. They experience a deeper peace. They have more gratitude for the Presence of God in their lives. It's not how subtle or loud the message is, it's how clearly it is received and implemented that makes such an impact.

His suggestion? Take a common, everyday dry erase board, and with Molly begin to write down all the issues in our marriage; all those things we wished and prayed to be rid of, erasing each one, multiple times if necessary, until it was fully erased from our hearts and lives. Then, on the other side of the board, my wife and I were to fill it with those qualities we truly wanted to manifest, writing each one down as a foundation of our renewed covenant. That was it. Simple, brilliant, perfect.

I felt hope well up in my heart for the first time in awhile. If Molly was willing to try it, there just might be a chance it could work. The retreat could have ended at this point and I would have been content, but my heart was still not conditioned to accept the healing I was being offered by the Divine. The puzzle was still not complete. There were two more crucial components needed before I went home to share my gift.

First, I was given the gift of remembrance. During an inner contemplation, Prophet took me back over every year of my marriage. With incredible clarity and detail, I was able to view my actions and regrets with kindness and understanding. Rising above the harsh emotional and critical viewpoint, I was able to disentangle from my emotions. To look at something directly and clearly without judgment is such a wonderful perspective to view life.

The second gift was delivered when I sang HU together with the class. During the sacred love song to God, I put all of my cares, hopes, and dreams for my marriage on the Altar of God. I had sought to put God first in all areas of my life, but in my marriage I had not. I had put *me* and *my* wants first. Now I truly saw Molly as the Divine being she is. I wanted her to be happy. If she was happier without me then I was okay with that.

From this place of surrender came such freedom, like I have never experienced before, and in that freedom I felt a peace that seemed supernaturally solid and unshakable. I had previously experienced what is described in the Bible as a peace that surpasses all understanding, but this peace felt even greater! I would give all to maintain this. I surrendered to the Divine anything that was not my direct relationship with God and His Prophet. How I looked. How well I did in life and my spiritual path (or thought I did). My marriage. My children. I gave up everything but my love for God and the precious relationship with the Divine that sustained and nurtured it. With this inner peace I was now experiencing, I was okay. The space in my heart, opened by Prophet's unwavering guidance and love, was now filled.

I look back now and wonder if the peace was really different than what I had experienced before, or if I was now so different and more receptive that I accepted and experienced God's peace on a whole new level.

Regardless, my heart was now ready. With my priorities put back in their proper order – God first, then my marriage – I felt confident all would work out for the best, whatever it looked like.

When I arrived home, my excitement to share this gift from God trumped any worries or concerns I had. I explained to Molly what I wanted to try. After the kids were in bed I brought out the dry erase board and wrote down a couple of issues I was ready to let go of. My wife looked on, poker-faced. When I finally wrote down something I knew Molly would be thrilled to see gone, I watched her initial reluctance disappear, and she joined me in naming and then surrendering, one by one, the hurt and pain. One by one we gave name to the enemies and wiped them away.

The results were stunning; greater than I could have hoped for. Every issue written down and erased seemed to lift almost immediately, like the Hands of the Divine scooped it off our shoulders and out of our lives. These were things we had spent hours, weeks, and years discussing endlessly to no avail, yet they seemed to melt away almost before we had written them on the board to erase them. For several hours that night, and for the next several days, we continued to write these things down, slowly weeding them out of our lives. We had both prayed and tried and now, in God's timing and Grace, they were being removed.

Later in the week when we finally felt there was some room in our marriage and in our hearts again, we turned the board over for the second part of the exercise. We began adding the things we wanted to cultivate in our marriage: To help one another become the best we can be spiritually, to be a harbor of love for one another, to demonstrate our love and respect on a daily basis, but it was more than just a rote exercise. It was as if the Hands of God were filling us up with these Divine qualities our hearts wanted to manifest.

Accepting the Gift

A gift from God is primarily delivered by the God-chosen Prophet of the times. This is an important aspect of the Prophet. He decides when and if our hearts are right, and ready, to receive the gift God has for us. He also chooses the best way to deliver the gift. Knowing this makes me doubly grateful for every gift received. I know it is a blessing from both the Heavenly Father and from His Prophet, but receiving it is only part of the process. Opening and accepting the gifts are our responsibility and opportunity. It is doing our part, but we are never alone in this process. We have help.

Another blessing of having a living teacher with a physical body is help in understanding and accepting God's gifts to us. After all, who is better qualified than the one who helped deliver them! A portion of retreats at Guidance for a Better Life are spent sharing and understanding the gifts God has blessed us with. Why were we given what we were given? The gifts are always specific and the timing is always perfect whether we recognize it or not. I remember making the transition over a period of years from simply seeing a flash of light, to recognizing it was God's Light, to recognizing God was demonstrating His Love for me. It is a process, and becoming more fluent in the "Language of the Divine" helped me to first recognize and remember the gifts, then understand and appreciate them. Prophet used the analogy of gifts left unopened under the Christmas tree. Leaving them unopened or just with the wrapping torn off before moving on to the next gift might make an impression for a little while, but it probably is not going to be life changing.

A month after that gift class, my marriage had been transformed. Issues were still being resolved by little more than reverently having a conversation in front of the dry erase board. It was incredible. Through the next several months, Prophet continued to help me open these amazing gifts.

At a retreat in late December, I got the opportunity to share my experience with the rest of the class. Verbally declaring out loud how Prophet had blessed my marriage and the many healings that had occurred over the past year had a big impact. Up until that moment it was like a dream, but sharing it made the healing sink to an even deeper level. When I detailed the individual blessings of the past year, my appreciation grew and the individual puzzle pieces came together to form a bigger picture of God's demonstration of His Love for me.

At a second retreat early in the new year, I got another opportunity to share with the class. This was an opportunity to help myself. If I could not explain it again clearly, if I had allowed it to fade in my mind and heart, then I had stopped doing my part in the healing process. A spiritual healing can be undone. It was like a follow-up visit with the surgeon who had performed the operation. Fortunately, I was able to express the experience which was still vivid in my consciousness, even adding a few nuances I had not clearly explained before.

Later at that retreat, I got the opportunity to help another student by sharing some of the lessons of my experience which overlapped a part of their life where they were struggling. For Prophet to use my life lessons in some small way to help another Soul was remarkable to me. I felt very much like the parable of the cracked pot whose imperfections were used by the Master to bless others. This was still another layer to the healing. As Soul, it is my Divine nature to give. The opportunity filled me with immense joy.

In March, my wife and I were finally able to go away for what we considered our official honeymoon. Eight years earlier we had married quietly in a courthouse before a justice of the peace. There was no celebration with friends or family, and we were initially reluctant to even tell others. We did not even plan a honeymoon. Before long there were children; time and resources were tight. Not going on our honeymoon became simply another casualty of a growing list of regrets between us.

Now however, we were truly able to celebrate our marriage. We chose a weekend at a historic bed and breakfast we had visited over two hundred years ago in a previous lifetime together. Whether it was completely conscious or not, we were revisiting our past only instead of being bound by regret we were now ready to celebrate the incredible blessings that had been delivered with the utmost care and exacting precision by Prophet.

The highlight came on the morning we were ready to go home. We found a quiet spot near a lake. I truly felt like a newlywed as we basked in the gratitude of our memories. We sang HU and thanked God and His Prophet for the love, blessings, and grace that had been poured over us. In the blissful silence that followed I contemplated on the phenomenal changes that had occurred in a seemingly short time. Excitement and relaxation had replaced life-stealing stress and hurt. What a blessing a healthy marriage was!

Later, as the sun rose high over the lake I started to take selfies of the two of us. Like many parents, we took tons of photos of our children over the years, some with one of us with the kids, but almost none of the two of us together. Yet here we were, joyous and playful, taking silly, timed photos. It dawned on me something Del had said: As we grew we needed to take new internal photos of how we saw ourselves because the old "photo" no longer fit us. I realized that this was exactly what we were doing.

I also recognized an awake dream as we walked the grounds before we left. The majority of buildings, though done in the traditional Southern style, were still somewhat modern. The only building I was aware of that would have been present in our previous lifetime was the remnants of a small building that was now little more than piles of brick and stone. It had basically been reduced to rubble by time. So too had the pain and karma of our past been reduced to mere rubble. Compared to the "new" solid structures of our love, the rubble of our past was not at all daunting, nor did it seem insurmountable any longer. The walls between us had finally come down.

Right With God

"The days of any religion or path coming between me and my children are coming to an end" saith the Lord

December 29, 2013

The above quote is found at the beginning of all of Prophet Del Hall's books. In those words I see an awake dream. My wife and I were married December 29, 2006. As Prophet is bringing down walls between God and His children, he also brought down the walls in our marriage. Our anniversary is a celebration of God's Love for us. For He loves us so that He blesses us with a Prophet of the times. There is always a Prophet on Earth with a physical body. In the Prophet, God gives us the Light of the World so we may never be alone nor in darkness.

My marriage is not perfect. Neither am I or Molly perfect, but we are right with God. That makes all the difference in the world. We accepted the love, correction, guidance, and teachings of Prophet. Doing so conditioned our hearts to receive more truth, healings, and love. Abundance and peace have followed.

We still have room to grow in our marriage. As Del often says, "There is always more." Molly and I are still receptive to more growth, learning, and healing. I find it easier now to get over things, to quickly find the best resolution available, and move on. Conversely, I find it harder to settle. If something can be better, I find the courage to speak up in a way that is more respectful and loving. Marriage is sacred; Molly is a gift from God. How could I give any less than my best, less than all I have to give? Del once told me to never waste a single day. I had already wasted so many, years in fact. Years that seemed painfully hopeless; where a single day did not come close to fulfilling the measure of blessings God intended when we committed to be married. I find motivation every day to see past the grit that makes life more vibrant and challenging and to recognize the beautiful blessings Molly brings to my life. Having a day that falls short of perfection in no way diminishes the sacred promise we have made to God, to ourselves, and to each other.

Del has certainly taught me so much about how to love, but what amazes me is how much he has also taught me about how to live. Mistakes, imperfections, and a past we are not proud of do not have to keep us from the blessings God has for us. It is not too late to begin today. You cannot relive the past, but you can recapture the present. Live today like it is your last!

We are Divine beings and we are here to learn about love. These are two truths Del has taught me. Love *is* demonstration. It is doing, and it has two parts, to give and to receive. Both are skills that take lifetimes to sharpen and nurture. Putting God first has made my marriage and my life infinitely better. My sacred, unbreakable relationship with God and His Prophet has made my prayer a reality.

Written by Chris Comfort

2

Never Give Up on Love
Molly's Story

A Child's Promise to Her
Future Children

I made a promise to myself many years ago. My parents were going through a divorce at the time, and my world and heart felt like they were falling apart. Divorce has impacted many, whether by choice as an adult or by circumstance as a child, but nevertheless it still hurts. So at age seven I declared I would never, ever get a divorce. I did not want my own children to go through the same heartache I experienced.

Life has a way of testing us and bringing us right to the edge in order to know our true priorities and values. Little did I know then that this determination was better focused on not letting anything come between my inner marriage with God's current Prophet, but over time I learned. When we put God first then all these things shall be added unto us. This is my story of how God blessed and transformed my marriage through His Prophet, my teacher, Del Hall. These blessings allowed me to have a marriage that has not only survived but come to a place where it is truly thriving and continuing to grow in love. I am so grateful that God helped me to not only keep my promise but to give me more in my marriage and life than I could even dream of.

Childhood Blueprint

I am blessed to have two parents who love me. They did their best to demonstrate this, but like everyone they had their issues. Both were following their own childhood blueprints into adulthood, carrying on for generations issues rooted in the past, yet I am responsible for my own inadequacies and issues, not my parents. God knows our strengths and weaknesses and places us in the perfect family environment to grow. I am grateful to both my parents for what they have taught me and the experiences and support they have blessed me with.

I grew up thinking I was a victim of my

circumstances. In the early years of becoming Del's student, I learned an important pearl of truth: I am Soul, and Soul is not a victim. Accepting this has changed my life. Seeing ourselves as victims paralyzes us from making better choices now, and gives away our freedom as a spark of God. Ultimately, we are responsible for our own life and our attitude towards it. That being said, our past can and does influence who we are today, for better or for worse. Understanding my own past lives has helped me to see and follow breadcrumbs that have led me to who I am today. With Prophet's help, I have recognized patterns and traits that were not created in just one life.

My family moved to Europe when I was two. At the time, I was the youngest of three children. Later I learned that my mother had not even wanted to move there. She sank into a deep depression and battled loneliness in a foreign land. My parents' life seemed built upon fixing up and repairing our old farmhouse and the surrounding gardens. We had a menagerie of animals and canals to boat in. In many ways, it was paradise for an adventurous, animal-loving child, but when the renovations were complete, their marriage was too. My parents separated in 1986 when I was seven years old and my father chose to remain in Europe. For him, keeping our childhood home was important.

My mother decided to bring us back to America and ended up settling down in Virginia. She is a determined and self-reliant woman – survival qualities that are essential for a single mother. She worked many odd jobs, adding to my father's child support, in order to provide for our needs. We still always had extra, and she sacrificed her own needs to meet ours, but emotional instability plagued most of my childhood.

I was a sensitive child and my parents' unhappiness affected me. They had extremely different ways of handling life and its stresses, and I followed in their footsteps. As a result, I frequently found stability and comfort in being alone even though at some level I knew I was not really alone. I recall sitting in our playroom once when I was about six and curling into God's Loving Presence and feeling safe and secure in a time when my outer structure was unstable. As I lay there crying, "It" knew my heart without me even having to speak, and "It" comforted me on such a deep level. I recognize now that God had allowed me to experience the presence of His Comforter just when I needed it. Now as an adult I have come to know that this presence is always with me. Being aware of Prophet's presence throughout my day has brought a security like no other.

I can now recognize a lot of the blessings I took for granted as a child; traveling to foreign countries, food on the table, shelter, clothes, two parents, and siblings who loved me. While these blessings influenced who I am, they did not provide the security that God's Presence does. Over the past fifteen years of being Del's student, I have learned that my insecurity and other inner ills have older roots than just this lifetime. God had created the perfect circumstance in this life for it to come to the surface and be dealt with. Even with the hurt, it was all a blessing and opportunity to learn and grow.

Echoes of the Past

My grandfather unexpectedly left my grandmother when my mother was barely two and her little sister was an infant. Understandably, this made a huge impact on my grandmother. She had to provide emotional as well as financial support solely for her daughters at a time, the 1940s, where there was a big social stigma for being a single mother. So my mother grew up in an environment where there was a distrust of and disrespect for men.

My mother took a liking to the mentality of the 1960s and considered herself a strong-willed feminist. No man would tell her what to do. Her attitude was that she could do anything she felt like doing. Life was run on emotion. A bumper sticker on her car once said a woman without a man is like a fish without a bicycle. These attitudes permeated the air as I grew up.

On the other hand, my father was more passive emotionally and soft natured. He grew up the eldest in a nuclear family of five where intellect was strongly nurtured and encouraged. Being logical, emotions were better left buried inside where they wouldn't rock the boat. Isolating one's needs, as well as being rational and stoic, were considered virtuous. Problems were not really talked about unless they had a scientific and mathematical solution.

Kind of an interesting combination God had for me. The loud, outspoken feminist and the quiet, stoic man.

Loving From a Distance

My siblings and I spent the school year with my mom and visited my father every summer for two months. Having to love my father from a distance hurt a lot. I remember falling asleep many nights just wanting to be tucked in by him. I spoke with my father on the phone every Sunday. He visited a few times a year and his loving support was there, but I missed his physical presence. So I built walls, and fortified them. I didn't really want to let anyone in again.

Most of the year involved missing my father but pretending I didn't. I knew he missed us terribly. I learned to pretend I was fine, thinking I was protecting him from feeling sad, but deep down I was insecure. Was I really loved? Why wouldn't he want to be closer to us? I had a lot of questions I was afraid to ask.

Nevertheless, I put my father on a pedestal and idolized him. He rarely disciplined me when we were together since it was like being on vacation, and I was on my best behavior. This made it challenging for me to accept criticism or correction as an adult. I falsely thought that I was "perfect."

Ironically, when I pretended to be a grown-up, my daydreams did not usually involve weddings and a husband – just lots of kids. I had been taught from an early age that I was stronger if I didn't need anyone, especially a man. Showing that you needed someone was weakness. Being vulnerable emotionally was worse. Controlling others became for me a way to avoid both.

A New Reference Point

Growing up, I didn't have any reference for what a happy marriage even looked like. This changed when I met Del and his wife Lynne in 2001. During the several months I interned at retreat center in 2002, I recall being surprised at how she would cheerfully and willingly find ways to serve and give to him. How she treated him with respect. Not that he was above her, but that she would willingly follow his lead. She would yield to him and what he wanted, putting him first.

She genuinely seemed happy finding simple ways to make his life better – like walking down the mountain terrain to bring him his forgotten cup of coffee while he worked. She beautifully demonstrated love and devotion.

He would openly express appreciation and affection to her. He clearly cherished and loved her, demonstrating it by how he spoke to and treated her. Their love for one another was, and is, palpable. They were clearly glad to be around each other. This was a foreign concept to me. I hadn't seen love like this before. As I have come to know and observe them more over the years during retreats, their marriage continues to inspire me as to what is possible: a heavenly marriage on Earth.

A Touch

Chris and I had known each other as fellow students at Guidance for a Better Life for several years. Both of us had been in previous relationships when we met, but in the fall of 2004 we were both single and independently attended a spiritual seminar in Minnesota. Along with twenty or so mutual friends from Guidance for a Better Life, we met after a full day of workshops and speeches to hang out, eat some snacks, and chat. We gathered in a small hotel room with friends seated everywhere; on windowsills, beds, and the floor. I found a spot leaning against the door, enjoying the banter and conversations. Chris was seated in front of me, propped underneath the snack table. I remember being endeared by this slightly unusual behavior, recalling how as a child I used to love sitting under tables and listening to adults talk. I surmised that he must be comfortable in his own skin to do that in front of other people, even if he was just trying to find a sitting spot in the small, crowded hotel room.

Then something stirred in me. I looked at him, the back of his head actually, and a wellspring of deep love came forth. It was like God was opening a curtain and allowing me to see what was really in my heart for this man. I was totally surprised by it. He was attractive and handsome, but I had never thought of him as my "type." Now my heart was overflowing for him. It was the first time in this life I had felt this way towards anyone. I knew that I loved him deeply. It actually kind of startled me. For several years I had been learning at the retreat center and experiencing at home that good things happen when I follow my heart (Soul) but this? I didn't really know him.

I knew the box of what I thought I liked, and he didn't seem to fit in it. He lived in a big city, shaved, and worked as a computer tech. Not in my box of the bearded, dirty finger-nailed farmer that I thought I wanted, but God knew better. My box was so small that love couldn't even fit in it. God wanted more for me, true love.

I almost overrode the inner prompting I was receiving from Prophet to reach out and touch him, but I had begun to learn the blessing of following those inner nudges from the Divine. So I did. The love flowed from my heart into my hand and onto his head, and he felt it. Later he said his head tingled for days afterward. I credit that to having already been ordained by God to touch others with His Love. In that moment, my love was intertwined with God's Love for Chris.

I will remember that evening, the moment where I was first given remembrance of loving Chris, my now husband. When he turned to look at me, the love in his eyes startled me. Clearly, I hadn't thought past the touch. I can laugh about it now, but I didn't feel ready. I felt safer hiding in my box. I had been avoiding being vulnerable to anyone since I was seven. Now with just him looking at me, I felt totally vulnerable as if he could see right through me. He would eventually find out I wasn't perfect, and my faulty self-image would be shattered.

He contacted me via e-mail a few days later. In a lighthearted way, he shared how he had felt a lot of love in my touch, joking that maybe I was just pulling a Cheetos out of his hair. I don't recall my exact response, but essentially I blew it off. I felt so defenseless with him, and it scared me. My whole life, even with friends, I had been distant. I had moved a lot as a young adult. I was good at making new friends but not as good at deepening the friendships I had.

God knew what was in my heart and lovingly gave me time to accept it. My heart felt drawn to Chris, but I didn't have the courage to follow it. Yet.

Meeting My Husband in a Dream

A few months after the seminar, I was given a dream in which I do not recall any words being spoken, but what was said through a glance altered my life more than any other dream I have had. In the dream, Prophet was standing before me looking at me with so much love. I trust him immensely. Ever since I first heard Del's voice on the phone in 2001, I knew I could trust him. Soul recognizes truth. Now fifteen years later, that initial knowingness has proven to be true time and time again. A living Prophet has a physical incarnation with physical limitations just like you and me. The faces and personalities of true Prophets of God change, but the same eternal presence flows through them. This makes my love and trust with the current Prophet even stronger. Our Divine relationship is not just from this life; it has been built over many lifetimes.

In this dream, Prophet stepped to the side. Chris stood before me with love in his eyes. In the silent moment between us, Prophet brought us together in this life. I knew in that unspoken moment that Chris and I had loved each other many times before. What Prophet lovingly shared without words was, "Here is someone whom you love and someone who loves you dearly too."

When I awoke from this dream, I knew that Chris was the one, but it is one thing to know something with certainty and another to have the courage to follow it. This dream had given me the courage to reach my hand out to Chris again. I didn't know what would come of it, but I knew that following Prophet's guidance would lead to a blessing. So this time I emailed him, asking if he wanted to come for a visit. A few weeks later, Chris and I went on our first date. This has become part of our history, twelve years and three beautiful children later.

Our story didn't begin with this dream it began many lifetimes ago. For me, the dream gave me a remembrance of what once was, and a premonition of what could be, all in the eyes of

Prophet and my future husband. While I did not decide to marry Chris based on this one dream, it was definitely the threshold that opened my eyes to recognize him as the man I love.

As eternal beings, the love connections we share with our loved ones span beyond space and time. We are reconnected with those we love because we are so dearly loved by Our Heavenly Father. We are given opportunities to heal past hurts and celebrate the joy of life together again.

Here is where a fairy tale ending would have us begin; dating, get married, and live happily ever after, but our story was not that simple. Our love was surrounded by unresolved hurts. Chris and I are aware of at least five past lifetimes in which we knew and loved each other. There are probably more we are not yet aware of, and while our love grew over time, unresolved issues grew with it. The love was clearly there between us, but even our initial courtship was rocky and turbulent. This continued well into our marriage.

Love Doesn't Fit in a Box

My early dating years involved mostly distant relationships, either physically or emotionally.

When I met Chris in my mid-twenties, he was different. He was very present emotionally, not distant at all. Where I feared emotional intimacy, he loved and relished it. He was intense and passionate in expressing himself. While this was a relief that helped me break out of my rigid expression of emotions and love, it also deeply intimidated me. I felt inadequate to express myself, especially to someone who had a way with words and expressing how he felt. I felt like a clumsy toddler trying to communicate with a linguistics professor.

He poured his heart out to me, and while deep down I loved every minute of it, I pushed it away. I didn't believe it could last, even though deep down I wanted to be with him for the rest of my life. True love was knocking on my door and peering over the walls in my heart, and I was afraid to open it.

But Chris wasn't giving up, nor was God. I am so grateful that they both loved me enough to give me the time to accept and open the gift.

Unhealthy Habits

Chris dove head and heart first into our relationship, ready to marry me and have kids after a month of dating. While I knew that God had blessed me with insights of the love that we shared and that Chris was incredibly charming, funny, and perfect for me, I was timid and wanted to go slower. Part of this was due to my inability to accept so much love directly from another. My heart was just not ready.

Thanks to my teacher Del, I had been traveling into the Heavens and experiencing more of God's Love from the Divine, but accepting love person-to-person was still something that was hard for me. Deep down I didn't feel worthy, so I pushed Chris away in the only way I knew how. I sowed uncertainty, and I treated him with disrespect.

It was almost like I was unconsciously putting him through a battlefield test to see if he would remain loyal to me, throwing all kinds of trials his way. He more than proved his love for me but at a high price. In those early years, I focused more on my own issues and doubts than on his needs. I was self-centered and didn't give him the love and security he deserved and needed. Thinking about myself was incredibly unsatisfying, and even though I had love in my life, I was not enjoying it.

Being with him, I was facing myself for the first time. I did not know yet that these inner ills that surfaced, the anger, lust, and vanity, were not the real me. At the time I identified with them and thought these issues were really me. It took many more years of healings from the Divine and identifying with my true self as Soul, before these began to lose their grip.

Even though I logically knew teachings from Del about the condition of our hearts, I didn't fully apply what I was learning in my own life. I had heard Del say many times there is only so much room in our hearts, and if we hold guilt, anger, or vanity we have less room for love. I felt confined by my selfishness and insecurities, and wasn't free to just be. I would try to prove my love instead of just loving. It was a crazy cycle that I couldn't seem to stop. I could recite, "Gratitude is the secret to love," but I wasn't living it. Even though I knew Chris was a blessing I wasn't demonstrating it.

For years, I falsely felt safer not communicating even though he desperately wanted me to open up and share myself with him. The louder he talked, the quieter I got.

From the early days of our relationship we were going around and around the same mountain. I had a dream that demonstrated this very experience a few years into our marriage. In it, we were under a roof. We couldn't see up, and there was some sort of maze in front of us. Chris and I kept circling and circling around the same location, never able to get to the center of the maze, nor out of it. Occasionally we would find a way out but then around and around we would go again. It mirrored our waking life precisely. Arguments and issues between us seemed to keep going around and around, becoming more and more embedded. We could never seem to get to the place of resolution, or being able to put a period on issues – emotional, financial, or social.

I felt almost helpless to make a lasting change. His frustration was evident too. Occasionally, we had windows of happiness. I remember those breaths of fresh air so fondly. We shared and appreciated each other and enjoyed the gift of being parents together. I really respected his role as our children's father and admired how loving he was, and is, with them. Those moments of relative peace would leave me asking, "Why can't it always be like this? We clearly love each other. Why do we keep going back to the old ways of relating?" Most of our issues were rooted in the past, taking us out of the moment. I prayed many times for a clean slate so the love between us could just freely flow, but then something or someone would unintentionally trigger a past hurt. And around and around we would go again.

Learning How to Express Love

During a winter retreat a few years into our marriage, Chris and I received help from the Prophet after sharing a little about what we were struggling with at home. Del insightfully shared that we didn't know how to express the love that we felt for one another. Our ways of relating were mostly out of habit and we needed to help each other keep our hearts open. If one of us could recognize the other person's sensitivity and help reassure them we could transform our ways of relating. This rang true.

Del's advice helped us. It gave us the breathing room we desperately needed, but over the course of the next two years, we slowly allowed the unresolved hurts to creep back in. Fight by fight, our hearts closed a little. Guilt, regret, and anger were seeping in again.

In hindsight, it wasn't God's time yet. We still had more room to grow individually before the love could freely be given and received between us. Over the following years we continued to attend retreats and were blessed with experiences of Divine love. Our hearts were being conditioned. God had a plan for our lives and my trust in this helped me get through the storms.

Slowly, with Prophet's help, I started to take responsibility for my actions and make different choices in how I treated Chris. I didn't want to live with regret, and Prophet was helping me. I could see the glimmer of a new cycle. I didn't have to repeat the history of disrespect. This opportunity was a gift from God.

Over these years, there were many insights, healings, and blessings I received from Prophet. Each of these has been a piece in the puzzle of my growth and unfoldment as Soul. And while some of them are easy to remember and treasure, others are stored in my heart. All of them nurtured and built a strong and solid foundation of the truth that God loves me. Accepting this truth has changed my life and given me the true security that only God and His Prophet can. This security changed how I related to Chris.

A Dream of Reassurance and Encouragement

About seven years into our marriage it was even more turbulent. We fought a lot, a cycle I wanted to change but hadn't. I felt discouraged and was starting to lose hope. Then I had a dream that became a raft for me to hold onto. In it, I was in a classroom at a heavenly temple. Prophet was teaching us about love and marriage. He said, "Some marriages can't ever work out," referring to a friend who had recently separated from her husband of many years. Prophet was giving her the confidence and reassurance that she had made the right choice to end her marriage. "But in other marriages the healing takes time, so don't give up" he said.

These words were directed at me. I felt relief and reassurance hearing this, and I awoke with a sense of encouragement. I wrote the dream down in my journal, knowing that I would refer back to it. This became one of those dreams that has stayed with me, giving me solace just when I need it. I didn't need my journal to remember his words: "Don't give up, healing takes time."

The timing of this dream was impeccable. At the time, our three young children were a stable love connection that we deeply enjoyed together, but in our marriage we were not growing closer. Both of us, no matter how hard we tried and how motivated we were, could not seem to shake the negative habits which were ingrained in many of our interactions. I had planted seeds of uncertainty early on in our relationship and could not remove them from my beloved's heart.

From guidance on the inner from Prophet and insights at retreats, we had returned to each other many times motivated to make changes and make things right in our marriage. We read many marriage books and listened to marriage tapes. We spent hours and days and weeks trying to fix things between us. In our efforts to improve our relationship, we focused a lot on what was wrong and on ourselves. This was a downward spiral. It seemed like the harder we tried, the worse it became. We were living in the past, not in the present.

Over the years, these small oases we reached in our relationship made it seem like we were making progress in expressing love and living true to our shared goals, but then we'd step back. I found this emotional roller coaster extremely exhausting. I began isolating myself from my friends. We were both unhappy with how things were between us and ultimately with ourselves. This affected every area of our lives.

This dream became a sanctuary for me. Sometimes even in the midst of an argument, I would find refuge in Prophet's promise: "Healing would come, it just takes time," but I didn't know how much longer I could wait. The regret I carried with me daily was eating me inside. Those "if onlys." If only I hadn't sown insecurity. If only I hadn't pushed away. If only I hadn't been selfish. If only I had expressed respect and reassurance to him.

Being Conditioned to Accept Blessings

Throughout our courtship and marriage Chris and I continued to attend retreats at the retreat center many times a year. Attending retreats and learning from the Prophet of our times was, and is, a precious and essential part of our lives. Each retreat we attend blesses us. Sometimes the changes are minor and sometimes we experience a major transformation.

We were being conditioned as Soul in Prophet's presence each time we came to the retreat center. This was stirring and activating our innate qualities as Soul that had been mostly lying dormant within us. We received healings, insights, and experiences that were bringing other aspects of our life into greater alignment with God and blessing us, but our marriage was still mediocre at best.

This changed by our each attending one retreat. It had been a puzzle of perfect timing from God over years and years. In fact, I believe God had set it up for lifetimes to be a success now. Chris and I had the opportunity to each attend a retreat in the fall of 2014. I went in October and he in November. I consider these our gift classes. They put the crucial pieces of the puzzle together so we could love one another again with a clean slate - as Soul.

The Gift Class

Over the course of that precious October weekend, God gave me tailor-made experiences that fortified the Divine part of me, Soul. After singing God's ancient name HU, I had the blessing to travel spiritually to a sacred temple with Prophet. While I had been fortunate to experience this many times before, this was the retreat in which the teachings really started to click in my heart. It was a turning point for me spiritually. I more fully experienced and accepted who I am: a Divine spark of God whose true nature is peace. Seeing this, I knew my life needed to reflect peace and joy. I am a child of God, not a child of issues or anger or regret.

So as Soul, in a state of true surrender, I decided I wouldn't let my marriage erode my peace anymore. I had had enough. Not of Chris, but of the strife. I could no longer encumber myself with worry or stress over my marriage.

I was willing to let go of my childhood promise to myself, let go of what I thought was best for my children, and let go of this man whom I loved. I truly surrendered my marriage to God. I could let go now. Making the decision as Soul was a very important distinction for the change to be lasting and fruitful. I had wanted it to change before, prayed for it to change, but now I was willing to truly surrender it. I had done all I could. Now it was on God's Altar. His Will be done in my life.

The worldly connotation of surrender means defeat, but to spiritually surrender means placing our trust, confidence, and faith in a higher power. To yield to the Divine is a great joy. There is nothing like it. It gives freedom, all the while promoting true responsibility. Having security in God's Love for me allowed me to surrender to a deeper degree than ever before.

I knew that I was responsible for my side of our marriage and before the inner Prophet I accepted my part in its failure, but I couldn't feel guilty over it anymore. There was nothing I could do to change the past, but I could change my present, and as Soul I could change my attitude. This was a huge healing for me. I felt so free. If you have ever truly surrendered something in your life and placed it in God's Hands, you know the peace and freedom of which I speak.

Inwardly, I declared the truth that my inner marriage with the current Prophet of the times and my peace of heart were more important to me than anything. God was first in my life and would stay first.

I recognized what I had thought was love was actually mixed with entanglements and conditions: the ways I thought Chris should be, how I thought he should act, or how I thought our marriage should look. Letting all of this go was so freeing. Combined with this freedom came an incredible, deep love for Chris. I truly wanted to see him happy, and I was willing to give up what I wanted if it would make him happier. I returned home to my husband with a purer love for him as Soul. I truly wished him well, and now I was free to just love him, no matter what form it took. I trusted and let go.

My priorities were in alignment: God first, marriage second.

A True and Profound Healing

Less than one month later, God surprised and amazed me with a tremendous gift. Chris returned from a retreat with a mission and a tool that transformed our marriage on so many levels. He writes more about it in his part of this book. We call it the dry erase board.

In the process of writing down what we no longer wanted in our marriage, I felt Prophet's presence and God's Hand literally lifting the heartache and habits from our lives. This was not something we did. While we did our part to follow the Divine guidance from Prophet, the healing is all thanks to God and His chosen Prophet.

When Chris came home, I don't recall him saying that he too had truly surrendered our marriage and was putting God first from now on. He demonstrated it, though. He had a peace about him. This disarmed me. Where I had been guarded in past conversations, now I was open and receptive. With the dry erase board, I was willing to participate. I saw almost immediately how it was something that would bless both of us. Even that first night, there was a glimmer of a softening and forgiveness from him, a letting go of past hurts. This helped me to more fully forgive myself.

As we wrote things that we no longer wanted in our marriage and erased them with Prophet, I felt safe. I felt secure, not just in Chris' enduring love for me, but also in God's Love. My dream marriage was now becoming a reality. God and His Prophet had kept their promise, as they always do. And they had helped me to keep my promise.

It wasn't until a few months later when we were reminiscing and appreciating our transformation that we realized a key piece to our healing was mutual. By both of us putting God first, great things had happened. With God in the equation the sum is infinitely greater than its parts.

One of the key blessings that came for me personally with the dry erase board healing was the transformation in how I viewed my husband. I now have such a deep respect for him. He was following God and led our family in a Godly way. I had seen his efforts over the past ten years in trying to transform our marriage and make it better. He had never wanted us to settle for a mediocre marriage and had advocated for our love before, many times. Now his loving determination and reliance on God and His Prophet was bearing fruit.

The key component was that we had now both put God first, what a difference it made. Friends noticed how we were different with each other. Without sharing what we had experienced, our families noticed a softening in our faces and demeanor. We became more active participants in life, giving and sharing the love that began at home. Now that we were more right with God, and our home life was right, we had so much more love to give to others. This was an answer to one of the prayers we had placed on the dry erase board, an area we wanted to support and nurture each other. This was such a prayer being answered. As Soul, we were doing what we came here to do: To be an instrument for God and to give and receive love. There is such a joy and peace that comes from this.

Relaxing Gratefully

Part of the healing process involved a period of tremendous relaxation for me. I hadn't even realized how much stress I was carrying. It was such a stark difference to how we had been living – with weekly, if not daily, strife. I recall one night just crying in relief that the strife was gone between us. We were not created to be worried or stressed. It doesn't mean there isn't heartache or struggle down here, but we have help! We don't go through life alone, for God's Prophet is always here with us. I treasure knowing and experiencing this through the ups and downs of life.

I also began to like myself. I, Soul, am beautiful and giving. All of those issues that I once identified with no longer had a grip on me. I was free to just be myself – quirks, imperfections, and all. I was still loved by God, by Chris, and by myself.

My appreciation for God and Prophet grew tremendously during this time. The more I was opening my heart to Chris, the more open my heart was to God. What had once been a downward spiral had been transformed into an upward spiral. The more I appreciated, the happier I felt.

My appreciation and love for my children grew as well. I am so grateful for their presence in our life. Furthermore, I didn't have the lingering guilt that I was hurting them with the condition of my marriage. Recognizing that they could now witness a healthy and happy marriage was such a prayer answered. I was finally giving my husband the respect that he deserved. By God's Grace, the generational patterns had been stopped.

A Promise Kept

When Chris and I married at the courthouse in 2006 I promised him I would do my best to love and honor him for better or for worse. I kept my promise to him, and he kept his to me through good times and bad. Even more, God kept His promise to us to help us grow in giving and receiving love, and God kept His promise to send His Prophet to guide us home. Our marriage with the Divine helps and uplifts our marriage, and vice versa. Just seeing Chris or thinking of him opens my heart, and an open heart helps me to be more receptive to hearing God. Appreciation for the many ways Chris blesses my life does too.

Does this mean our marriage is perfect? We still have arguments from time to time, but the fights don't have us anymore. We can laugh in the midst of one, tease each other, and move on. Whether or not we disagree is no longer a qualifier for a "perfect" marriage. We don't close our hearts to each other, no matter what we are talking about. We remember that the other person is a child of God and worthy of love and respect. It is a marriage founded on God and love. That is perfect to me.

I want to do everything I can to keep my own heart right with God and love my amazing husband. No argument is worth losing sight of the blessing that he is to me.

Early on, I prayed for God to just take away the pain and strife, to fix it before I even understood it or my own culpability. I am so grateful that He answers prayers in His own way and with impeccable timing.

In God's way, I learned the confidence that comes from doing all we can and leaving the rest to God. I learned the value of truly surrendering to and trusting God and His Prophet. I learned that when we truly put God first, our life is truly blessed. I learned that with God's help and prolonged determination we can overcome obstacles.

"Never Waste a Day"

Last summer, Del shared something with Chris and me during a friends' wedding reception, "Never waste a day." He was referring to a photograph of Chris and me after our healing where I was just hugging him and we were both smiling. Every day can be that sweet and precious, he said. Having wasted many days in our marriage, I appreciate the love in his words even more.

The degree to which our marriage changed, thanks to the Divine and God's Prophet Del, was phenomenal. In some ways it is a new marriage, but in other ways, it is the one we always had that was just hidden underneath layers of pain. Thanks to God our hearts are now open to give and receive love between each other, our children, family, and friends.

What was once a dream is now my daily reality. None of this would be possible without the love, guidance, nurturance, and eternal teachings of Prophet. Our Father wants to shower us with blessings. Perhaps you have gifts He has already blessed you with, but have you truly opened them? Have you accepted the full measure of joy and happiness that God wants for you? I promise you there is more.

For me, my marriage with Chris exemplifies this very thing. I peeked in the box when God first showed me what was in my heart as I touched Chris's hair and looked into his beautiful eyes in my dream, but I didn't think I was worthy of that much love. So I didn't accept it. Over time, the walls and boxes around my heart began to break open by the Grace of God. He helped my heart be ready through the love and nurturance of His chosen Prophet at retreats and at home. Slowly, the hurt and inner ills were removed and healed. I came to realize and accept that I was worthy and very blessed indeed.

The more we recognize ourselves as Soul, the more life begins to reflect our true nature. A nature of joy, peace, freedom, and security in the eternal truth that GOD LOVES US. A wall that once stood between Chris and me has crumbled. So has the wall between God and ourselves - thanks to Prophet. We are so blessed!

God and Prophet, I truly appreciate the Love that you have poured over my life and into my heart. Your Love has transformed me from the inside out. I am so excited to continue to grow in my marriage, with You Prophet on the inner and with my beloved husband Chris. Thank you for believing in me and not giving up on me. Thank you for helping me keep my own promises. Thy Will be done in my life always. I love you.

Written by Molly Comfort

Summary – Chris and Molly

Our gratitude goes out to God and to Del and Lynne Hall, whose demonstration of putting God first in every area of their lives and of having a loving marriage inspired us to reach beyond the limitations of our past, to press on through challenges, and to more fully accept the blessings of God in our lives. We both feel that our message is one of hope and help. There are both in abundance, ready for you too at the perfect place and time.

Prophet blessed us with help, guidance, and healings. He also guided us through a series of opportunities to a place where we both surrendered all on the Altar of God. We both made a conscious choice to put God first. This was an incredible turning point in our marriage.

Once the conditions in our hearts were right we were able to accept and utilize the tools that God gave us to co-create a beautiful and abundant marriage. We did not just hear the advice, we did something with it. Accepting the Love of God means more than hearing good advice. It means accepting help beyond what we could have imagined and doing our part. The tools we were given were blessed by the Divine. Issues and pains of the past were healed that we could not heal ourselves.

The healing in our hearts and our marriage ended a cycle of divorce, hurt, and disrespect that went back many generations. Breaking this cycle has freed us, our children, and our future grandchildren from the bonds of this vicious pattern. The golden ripples will impact generations. For this and the Love of God, we are truly grateful.

Written by Chris and Molly Comfort

3

Here to the Ocean
Carmen's Story

When I was in the process of moving to Virginia in October of 2008, I had a thought that I might meet "the one." I began to call this future significant other my mountain man. I was moving to the mountains after all. It was a dream in my heart to meet a man I could love and who truly loved me. God read my heart and answered this prayer. I was reunited with a beautiful Soul whom I love dearly.

Some folks I am blessed to call my friends invited me out to dinner shortly after I moved. I pulled into the parking lot of a local grocery store near the restaurant. Also walking towards the restaurant was a very handsome man who struck up a conversation with me. We realized we had met briefly once before at Guidance for a Better Life during a retreat. We walked into the restaurant together. As the story goes, when we said goodbye I had to ask Mark to repeat his name because I forgot it. He took this as a sign that I did not like him. Let it be known this was not the case. I tend to forget names, and at that point would have never dreamed Mark would be interested in me.

It was not his gorgeous blue eyes that first stirred my heart. It was not his endearing smile or his easygoing manner. I remember the exact moment I was struck. I think God chose this time to bring the gift of remembrance to me. I was sitting next to him on the couch watching a DVD of a live Nirvana concert. I saw his feet there next to mine. He was wearing white socks. Our toes touched briefly and that was the moment I started to remember my love for Mark.

I say remember my love because it has been proven to me many times that Mark and I have loved each other before in lives long past and some not so long past. The love between us, as it began to dawn, was so strong and true. It was beyond the physical, rooted somewhere deep and beautiful.

Mark and I started dating in January of 2009 and were inseparable until we married October 15, 2011. On the surface it may not seem like it, but we have an arranged marriage. Our union was made possible by God, who brought us together in perfect timing. Our relationship with

Del Hall III, whom we lovingly know as Prophet, not only brought us together but helped us keep our marriage. We have been blessed to be students of the Prophet, attending retreats at Guidance for a Better Life as often as possible. At Guidance for a Better Life we learn more about giving and receiving love. We learn more about each other and our true selves, Soul. We also learn more about our sacred relationship with Prophet, which in turn brings Mark and me even closer together.

The Storm

A few short months after we were married a storm began to brew. I was hard to deal with. I was angry and emotional. I was like a puffer fish swimming along and then poof! Little spines like daggers were suddenly pointing out from all directions. It is hard to love a puffer fish, yet Mark did. Instead of focusing on the spines, Mark chose to see me as Soul. I am so appreciative of Mark's merciful attitude.

I lived my life most often in the defensive position, ready to strike out at the slightest hint of trouble. This was my norm. I was beginning to recreate some of the negative aspects of my childhood. It does not make it okay, but this is how I handled living in a house with a lot of yelling.

Back when I lived with my parents, I would pause outside the door to our mobile home, steeling myself before entering. I never knew what the mood would be like inside. I was on eggshells most of the time. I did not feel like I could measure up to the standard that was expected. As I got older, I developed a victim consciousness attitude. I later learned from Del that this attitude is poison to one seeking spiritual freedom.

When Mark and I were first married, I would rush around trying to make everything perfect before he got home. The house had to be clean, the dinner ready and on the table. I had to look presentable. These ridiculous standards were almost never achieved. If they were, I was a wreck with my stomach in knots and I could barely eat the dinner I had prepared. I was so uptight! Mark just wanted a smile and a kiss when he came home. He did not care if dinner was done or my hair was a mess. He loved me!

One might think all that rigmarole was just proof that I wanted to please my husband. I did want to please him, but I was so full of myself I had little room for Mark or for Prophet. Deep down I knew I was selfish, and I was asking for help. My prayers were answered then, and still to this very moment I continue to receive help from the Divine on selfishness. In fact, just the other day Mark came home and I noticed I was feeling a little uptight and uncomfortable. I went to the bathroom to put a load of laundry in and asked Prophet what was going on. When the answer came I laughed out loud. "Get over yourself!" he said. I instantly felt better and freer. I practically skipped out of the bathroom and had a wonderful evening with Mark.

God's Prophet Gives Truth

Six months after we were married I went to a special retreat at Guidance for a Better Life. It was a profound weeklong retreat with a small group of students. Prophet taught all week and brought us dreams at night that contained truth and wisdom from God. I had many dreams that week showing where I was at spiritually. Prophet was direct with me and shared the truth about how I was living. This week saved my marriage, my relationship with Prophet, and my spiritual life.

My life was abundant. Mark loved me and I

loved him. Mark built a beautiful house, and we were making it a home together. I had a good job, wonderful friends, and above all I had a sacred relationship with Prophet. All these blessings were gifts of love from God.

I was harboring attitudes in my heart that were becoming more and more apparent. I had a full pantry of God's blessings and I was dying of starvation because instead of focusing on the good I focused on what I did not have. This lack of gratitude turned into a hard heart and I lost sight of what was important.

I also had an attitude of entitlement. This entitlement attitude permeated everything I did. I was technically an adult, but I acted like a spoiled child, having fits when things did not go my way. In our marriage I felt entitled to certain things from Mark. I even acted this way toward God.

I was full of fear and worry. I was under the false impression that I could earn God's Love by doing more. I thought I should get another degree and then I would be happy. I felt like I was unsuccessful, yet I did not even know what success was for me. One of the biggest things that stressed me out when we were first married was thinking I had to bring home as much money as Mark. Because I did not really understand who

I was, I felt like I was not contributing enough and I was not enough. All these falsehoods made me a hard person to live with.

One dream Prophet gave me really hit home. I dreamt of Mark. His face was wrinkled and weathered. He looked pained like he had aged twenty years. He hugged me and said, "You are having a rough week. Get your head out of your ass." I woke from this dream with the understanding that Mark was worn out from dealing with me. When I came home Mark confirmed that he was tired of the way things were between us.

I was at a crossroads not only in my marriage but in life. I received many healings from God through His Prophet. I was given a prescription to focus on gratitude and take time daily for spiritual nourishment in a balanced way. Up until then I was more all or nothing on the spiritual path. I needed balance, focus, and discipline.

I am so appreciative of the truth and love Prophet gave me at the retreat. I was forgiven by Prophet and also by Mark. It took a long time to forgive myself and recuperate from the damage I had caused to our marriage. Being grateful was a golden key for me. When I am grateful I am blessed and so is Mark. A grateful person is full of love and this is a key component to be able to hear God's communication. I had so much fear, worry, and anxiety about life, I had very little real estate in my heart for love.

After Prophet gave me truth and guidance it took a long time but as I began to focus on and cultivate an attitude of gratitude things began to change for the better. Love was flowing in my heart again. I began to hear inspiration from Prophet about how I could improve and heal the damage that I had caused between Mark and me. This inspiration came to my awareness sometimes as a sudden clear idea that I knew was not from my mind.

This may sound silly, but I remember sitting on the floor upstairs in our bedroom folding clothes when an insight from Prophet came that I could start doing all the laundry. Up until then Mark and I both washed clothes, but after I received this suggestion I began to do all the laundry. I also started ironing his work shirts. I needed to give love and this was one way that I started. This small gesture was important because it demonstrated my love for Mark. The truth, as I began to accept it, was truly setting me free. Over time the storm I had brought on our marriage started to pass.

God's Promise of Children

There is a beautiful field on Del's property students are allowed to tent in during retreats. It was June of 2012, just three short months since that special weeklong retreat. I was sitting in a camp chair outside our tent enjoying the warm morning sun, my favorite time of day. I closed my eyes with the intent to connect with Prophet and express my gratitude to God. I was filled with appreciation for being right where I was, Heaven on Earth. I sang HU, a love song to God. In the quiet time afterward I had a vision that surprised and delighted me. I was in our backyard at home. God's golden Light shone down on a swing set. Children were playing and laughing. These were our children! I was shocked and elated. God would give us children? Did God really trust me to be a mother? This glimpse of a possible future was a huge part of the healing that God was bringing to my heart.

Up until this point when I thought of having kids I would react with fear. I did not trust myself to be capable of raising a child. To know God would trust me to be a mother proves that with Him anything is possible. God's Love in my life was transforming me. This was the beginning of being able to trust myself, too.

This prophetic gift marked the beginning of a most beautiful time in our marriage. It was filled with nights of talking, dreaming, and planning together. How did we want to spend our future? We were learning how to make conscious choices and "Create a life that worked for us," as my friend Roland so aptly said. Did we want to have a child? Just knowing God had blessed us by giving us the okay gave us confidence that our marriage was growing stronger.

A Healing Dream

I was standing in the middle of a huge room in a house that belonged to Mark and me. I knew it was ours, but it was as if I was discovering it for the first time. In front of me was a grand spiral staircase wide enough for three or four people to walk up side by side. Soft sunlight cascaded in from the home's many windows.

I was happy as I walked through seeing the potential that was there. The house was old but sturdy and in good condition. It was like an historic estate with nice details and lots of wood. My perspective changed to the ceiling, where I saw a slimy residue built up. It needed some work but it was worth restoring, and when it was done it would be gorgeous. My friends and family were all gathered inside, helping Mark and me renovate the house.

Later, as I was exploring, I discovered another wing. Two wooden French doors with glass inserts held back a new space. The room was lit with the glow of afternoon sunlight. Peering through the dusty glass, I was delighted to see a baby grand piano inside. Excitement coursed through me as I thought how beautiful this would be when it was finished. This section, I knew, was for the future. It was something we would open up down the road.

I awoke from this dream experience with a light, expansive feeling that filled my being. I knew the house represented my marriage to Mark. This dream came in the winter of 2012. Mark and I had been married a little over a year. Things were getting better, but I still doubted myself. There were moments when I wondered if Mark would decide he had made a mistake in choosing me to marry. This dream gave me reassurance.

While our marriage in this life was new, the love between us was not. Like this old estate, our relationship was enduring. It had and would continue to weather many seasons. Knowing that Mark and I were again, after lifetimes, restoring and growing in our love brought me strength. The home had some dirt and residue from the past, but it was just on the surface. Our marriage, like the estate, has a solid foundation. This helped me relax. It showed me that we were in a period of transition. Disagreements would come and this was okay!

Peace and gratitude filled my being. I understood that God, through His Prophet, was healing me through this dream. The experience filled my heart with love and began to push out the doubts and guilt I had created in the past. I had a renewed confidence that all would be well. The sunlight in the home was the Love of God. This love had brought Mark and me together again. God's Love would hold us together and sustain us forever. I also saw how much love and support we had from our friends and family.

Reflection upon this dream has revealed deeper layers that to this day continue to bring reassurance and peace to my heart. Prophet helped me understand this dream has many meanings. The estate, while representing my earthly marriage, was also a representation of my spiritual marriage to the Holy Spirit. Both of these marriages are sacred to God.

Secure in God

Mark and I were beginning to really enjoy each other again on a more regular basis. This began to transform how I related to Mark. I was able to set boundaries and started being able to truly trust and follow my heart. My mind has ruts and repetitive habits of reacting to protect itself, but the mind, as Prophet showed me, was not designed to run my life. It can crunch numbers, help me put my shirt on the right way, and memorize lots of data. Soul, among Its other attributes, can communicate with God, receive creative inspiration from God, and has a much higher view of life; and therefore better suited to be in the driver's seat.

I was now seeing with the viewpoint of Soul more often. The result was a lot less fighting between Mark and me. I felt secure in God's Love and could express my love more freely for Mark as a result. I was happier than I had ever been, and over time I actually began to like myself.

Growing secure in God's Love is a process that becomes deeper as my relationship with Prophet gets more solid. If I do not feel approved of by Mark or if I make a mistake, I know I am still loved by God. This balances me and makes me more stable emotionally. Prophet is always with me, guiding, and showing me the way of love. He has blessed me with the awareness of his presence. Choosing to live in his presence brings many blessings such as peace, clarity, joy, wisdom, and strength. I can then more freely express my love for Mark.

Again, this has been a slowly developing process. I still get worked up, but it is less than before and that is progress! Now I have a choice of how to be. Prophet taught me that I can choose how I react to things despite how I feel. Feelings can be fickle. I cannot always control my circumstances, but I can control my attitude and that makes all the difference.

Submitting to My Husband

While attending a retreat at Guidance for a Better Life we had just sung HU, a love song to God. In the quietude afterward, Prophet allowed me to kneel before him in a beam of God's Light and Sound. The Light shimmered gently. It was mostly white with soft glints of pastel colors here and there. Mark, as Soul, joined us in the beam of God's Light. I knelt in front of him and submitted to him in this sacred place before

Prophet. Then Mark knelt down and also submitted to me. No words were spoken. I just knew in my heart what was happening.

This was not something that had been in my awareness to do at the time, but it was so natural. Prophet helped me understand while in class and also contemplating with Prophet on the inner at home that it was an answered prayer and a healing too. Submitting to each other is very important for our marriage. It is the recognizing that Mark and me are joined before God. He is part of me and I am part of him. This is something I am growing in and I am excited for the journey.

I trust Mark with my heart. Mark is steadfast in his love for God and he follows God's Prophet. He makes good decisions and is a wonderful leader because he is "right with God." Mark is a true diamond of God. I love him and love being married to him!

Our Daughter

Our daughter is now almost seventeen months old. She got her first pair of shoes today. We handed her the little box which had a clear window so she could see what was inside.

"Shoes!" she shouted joyfully. I helped her get the shoes out and immediately she sat to try and put them on her feet. No sooner had the last pink strap been placed than she was squirming away and at the door. She stretched her arm as far as it could go and pointed at the door, "Outside!" Her whole body resembled an exclamation point the way she balanced on tip toes in her exuberance to try out her new shoes.

As I watched her in the backyard with Mark, I caught myself thinking in awe, "That is her, your daughter. She is actually here." Mark looked up at me with love in his eyes and a wide smile of delight as he watched her toddle through the grass. The setting sun blazed through our yard in a warm golden hue which reminded me of the vision I was shown by Prophet in the field at Guidance for a Better Life. There she is, God's Grace and Love in form and action. This sweet Soul is a dream come true to me and I love her.

Where there used to be doubt about motherhood, Prophet gave me confidence. Where there was anxiety, he gave me peace. Where I am weak, he is strong so the team is strong. Even though I was a mess in the beginning of Mark's and my marriage, I was not abandoned by God or His Prophet. I was allowed to go through the necessary lessons to learn and grow, with Prophet always there with me, guiding me. This is still the case now. I still make mistakes. I still have areas I can grow in and God still loves me. I thank you, Prophet.

A Renaissance Begins

Mark and I have begun to call this part of our relationship the renaissance period. As we have implemented the suggestions Prophet has made and followed his daily guidance as best we can, we are seeing welcome changes happening in our marriage.

One of the many blessings Prophet brought through our daughter is, the awareness of habits of thinking that deplete me spiritually. Not wanting to live with them or pass them onto her I decided to go see a doctor for counseling. I was finally not afraid to go. I used to think that if I needed to talk to a counselor I was somehow admitting defeat. It is actually a sign of strength to ask for help. God led me to the proper doctor and worked through her to bring clarity to my life.

From this experience I began to really understand the importance of forgiveness in relationships with people and God. It is vital for me to forgive if I want to clearly hear God's Prophet and feel his blessed presence. There were things that happened in the past which on my own I could not forgive. With Prophet's help and God's Grace however, I have been able to let go of long-standing hurts that seemed impossible to get over. One key to this has been Prophet showing me the part I played in some of these situations. Taking responsibility for my part seems to speed up the healing process.

Prophet also suggested Mark and I read <u>The Five Love Languages</u> by Dr. Gary Chapman. The book highlights five general ways people tend to express and want to receive love from their spouse. There is a test you can take to help you determine what your primary love languages are. It is a good starter kit to understanding your mate's needs, as there are more than just the five love languages covered in the book. The book helped me understand how Mark would best feel my love for him. Mark and I had both read it before, but this time as we read it spiritually with Prophet it really hit home. We were surprised at what our love languages were. I actually did not fully figure mine out but Mark did. I knew it was "quality time," but Mark realized that I specifically felt loved when he opened up to me and shared his feelings and thoughts.

He started to do this without my knowing it. When he started sharing how he felt, it made me feel closer to him in a different way than I had in awhile. Some of our earlier fights were due to this very topic. I would share how I felt too bluntly, too loudly, and too much. We would talk for hours with no resolution. I knew I was the one with most of the issues in our marriage. I was very insecure, and when I could feel Mark was holding back, my mind would make up all sorts of possibilities of why that could be.

Mark consciously chooses to share with me now, which I really love. I love talking with him and doing things together. I am making a conscious effort to verbally tell him how much I appreciate him. This helps Mark receive my love too.

Thank You Prophet

On our wedding night Mark and I lay next to one another on the bed. He rolled over and surprised me with a black velvet box. The inside sparkled in the dim light of our bedroom. It was a necklace and earring set in the unusual design of a thick golden triangle with two diamonds inside it. Mark explained that it was made specially for his grandmother Mimi by his grandfather. Mimi passed when Mark was in his early twenties. When asked if there was anything he would like saved for him, Mark asked his dad if he would save Mimi's necklace so he could give it to his future wife.

Mark explained that the diamonds were him and me inside God's Love. This means even more to us now. The golden triangle reminds us of our relationship with Prophet and God's Love. The diamonds remind us of Soul. I was so touched by this. It was a symbol and a foreshadowing of the potential our marriage has as two Souls united by God, standing on a foundation of God's Love. It also reveals the purity of Mark's heart and his intention for our marriage.

I thank you Prophet for your love. Thank you for bringing Mark and me together again and teaching us God's ways. I thank you God for my husband Mark. You teach me daily through him. He is patient, kind, loyal, trustworthy, and so much more. As Mark and I grow in giving and receiving love, our ability to demonstrate our love for one another becomes more refined. This would not be possible without you Prophet. I look forward to the years ahead. I love you.

Written by Carmen Snodgrass

4

Here to the Ocean
Mark's Story

If you are looking to hear about a couple who has marriage all figured out please skip this chapter. If you are interested in hearing about how God blessed a good marriage and gave us the tools and a chance to make our marriage even better then this might be for you. We feel we are in the beginning of a renaissance period within our marriage and feel God is truly trying to teach us what an abundant marriage is all about. God looked at our four years of marriage and then looked down the road, and by His Grace through His Prophet He chose to help us create a new future for our family and ourselves. Carmen and I both knew things could be better, and we wanted things to be better, but we did not know how. We were unable to break the cycles and habits we had brought into our marriage and were making them more and more permanent. It was our marriage, we created it and God knew it was not the marriage we both wanted deep in our hearts for each other and ourselves. We loved one another, that has always been constant and strong, but we had to learn to live together. The following is our story of how God's Prophet is helping us learn to express our love for each other and create the marriage of our dreams.

Our Beginning

Carmen and I met in January of 2009, and a week or so after our first date I got laid off from my job. This gave us a few months to really spend time together and get to know each other. I felt younger, more energetic, and happy around her. We enjoyed each other's company. It didn't really matter what we did, we just liked spending time together. By summer I had a knowing in my heart this was pretty serious and I wanted to spend the rest of my life with her. With this knowing came a peace I had never experienced before. I just knew this is what I wanted. Friends had told me I would just know when I met the Soul I wanted to marry, but I did not know what they meant until I experienced it for myself. I decided to give it a year to make sure we didn't rush into anything, but I had a feeling in my heart that I would still feel the same. I loved her. I did not have a particular reason why, as in past relationships, I just did. It was a knowing that seemed to go way back.

Over the next year our love grew, and the following summer I was ready to ask Carmen to marry me. I had prayed about the topic and continued to ask for guidance. Though I had peace and this knowing in my heart, I wanted to double and triple check that this was best for Carmen and me, and that our marriage had the blessing of God. I was then given an experience that confirmed what I knew to be true in my heart. I had saved for and purchased her engagement ring and decided I would ask her to marry me after we returned from a weeklong spiritual retreat at Guidance for a Better Life. During one experience Prophet was raising our group up spiritually and we got the opportunity to briefly visit twelve of God's Heavens, from planet Earth to God's great Ocean of Love and Mercy. As my physical body sat on the ground, I was able to travel in Spirit to experience myself in each Heaven. Starting with the physical, I checked if I truly loved Carmen and did I want to be married to her. I was able to ask this in the first Heaven, the second Heaven, the third Heaven and beyond, into the pure and higher Heavens where only God's living truth can exist.

I was greeted with and got to experience God's Love, peace, and reassurance, and a knowing that this is what I truly wanted. This experience seemed to grow within each Heaven, and my heart opened more in gratitude with each visit. Prophet took me all the way to the twelfth Heaven, our Heavenly Home. He and I were before God's great Ocean of Love and Mercy. I got to experience this part of me in my Heavenly Home before God and His Prophet. I knew all of me loved Carmen and that I wanted to spend my life with her. It was what I truly wanted and it was right with God. I love her from here to the Ocean. Thank you God for helping me see what is truly in my heart and giving me the peace and reassurance that goes with this. Thank you for bringing Carmen into my life.

Later that evening, Prophet took the group to one of God's great Temples of learning that can only be accessed in our spiritual bodies. During the experience we were given the opportunity as Soul to follow our hearts and explore this temple full of God's Love. I followed my heart to a special place in the temple garden and found Carmen spiritually before me. I got down on both knees and told her I loved her and wanted to spend the rest of my life serving God together side by side. I then asked her to marry me. She smiled and said yes and we were both very happy and full of joy. I reached out with both hands and gave her the diamond ring I had picked out and put it on her finger. We then spent time exploring God's Temple together.

I was reminded of an experience earlier that night where we got to look deep down into God's sparkling, golden-white Ocean of Light. I saw a beautiful diamond that sparkled beautifully. It seemed to dance, radiating the light and love of the Ocean. Looking deeper inside the diamond I saw it had a clarity and love that seemed to go on forever. I later realized the diamond represents me, Soul. It reminds me I am a jewel of God. This is how God sees me and wants to me to see myself. Each facet of the diamond is hand cut by God, and all our experiences make us a unique expression of God's Love. I realized I needed to give all of this diamond to Carmen, all of me, not just parts. Through this experience I was able to give her myself in Heaven, but I have discovered I also needed to share this with her daily. I have discovered Carmen is also a jewel of God. She is her own unique expression of God's Love and she should be treated and respected accordingly at all times. She is a gift from God to be cherished. I did not always treat her as such. I reflected back upon this Divine experience many times during our first year of marriage.

This experience gave me the strength to get through that first year. We fought a lot, and it helped me keep perspective of the big picture. I may not have known what was going on at the time, after the emotions of an argument turned us upside down and inside out, but I always knew I loved her and we made the right decision to get married. That has always been constant over the course of our marriage.

We loved each other, but the first few years of our marriage were hard on both of us. We had to learn to live together and to express ourselves differently than we had in the past. We have been given the opportunity to break family cycles that have existed for generations. We did not want to continue to live the way we had been.

Faulty Wiring From Childhood

I learned many good things growing up with my parents, and I know God picked good ones to help me learn and grow the traits I needed to develop in this lifetime. I must have needed to learn those lessons before I learned to express myself in a healthier way. All in God's time; God knows us well and God's timing is always perfect. My parents have been married now for over fifty years; not too many people around these days can say that. They found a way to live together over all these years. They seem happy now, but growing up it seemed like they were going to stay together regardless if either one of them was happy or not.

I grew up in a home where everyone seemed to be upset a lot of the time, but no one ever talked about it. Everything appeared fine, but the atmosphere in our home said differently. There was often an unspoken tension in our home. We did not talk about feelings. When things were bottled up for too long they were expressed in negative and sometimes heated and inappropriate ways, but not truly resolved. I learned that expression of my thoughts, feelings, and opinions was something best kept to myself.

When I was in my twenties, my mom and I learned to express our love verbally to each other, but I did not remember her telling me that she loved me growing up. I know now she loves me very much.

Later she shared with me that she could not remember being told verbally she was loved as a child either. She was raised that way and so was her father. It was very hard for her to express love in this way. Until then, I had no idea this was the case. I just wondered if she loved me. Her family expressed love in other ways but "I love you" to the children was not something said out loud. This was my mom's role model and she passed things on the best she could.

This created some quirks in my relationships and gave me insecurities that I was not aware of, one being the need for constant verbal reassurance from my partner. In past relationships and in my marriage, I could always say "I love you" and it genuinely flowed out of me. However to be asked to share my feelings sent panic through me. I did not feel comfortable sharing them. Growing up I learned to bottle up my feelings and emotions and at the same time feeling guilty for having them. Before meeting Del I did not feel good about myself and I was very numb emotionally. I remember at a young age my dad telling me I was not allowed to be angry. I think he meant well and was attempting to pass along some wisdom, as he saw many people waste a lot of their lives being angry and resentful, and that it was unproductive. Well, this comment made me angrier. I was not allowed to feel how I was feeling, but I failed to express this because we talked very little about feelings. So over time I learned to stuff down the anger and other feelings I really had, but felt guilty for having. It created quite the conundrum for me.

Dealing With Emotions Appropriately

God, through His Prophet, had healed me of many of these passions of my mind. I thought I had worked through most of my past issues. It is all relative, but I still have much more to learn: there is always more. So when I met Carmen I had insecurities and didn't know how to express myself very well. To keep the peace I kept things to myself and hoped they would work themselves out. My anger that had been in remission suddenly made its appearance again shortly after I met Carmen. The first few years of our marriage were rough and created tension for both Carmen and me. We both had to learn a new way to express ourselves, and how to give and receive love.

During a spiritual retreat in May 2015 at Guidance for a Better Life we had the opportunity to really look into our hearts and get clarity on what was inside. We were then able to receive additional help from Prophet. After singing HU, a love song to God, Prophet took us to the door of one of God's Temples. Once inside, we were given a great opportunity and got to ask ourselves if we wanted to continue to grow in our relationship with God. The answer for me was a very positive "Yes!" Later we were given another great opportunity. Prophet asked me what could he help me with? We were able to look into my heart together, but before I asked for help, I wanted to make sure I asked for something I really wanted. So I asked for help looking into my heart; and then asked the question "Did I still want to be married to Carmen?" I felt pretty secure but I wanted to ask the question. I wasn't afraid to ask: "Did I still want to be married to Carmen and continue to grow in our love and marriage?" I really wasn't attached to the answer. I wanted the truth more than anything in that moment, whatever it was.

With this truth came clarity and a freedom from the very question itself. The answer was a very positive "Yes!" I then experienced and felt the love and joy between Carmen and me as Soul. I also discovered we are even closer and that the bond between us is stronger than I realized. The truth was very freeing and also very reassuring. It is what I wanted and what we both wanted. I then proceeded and asked Prophet for help with our marriage, to help us communicate and express our love for each other better. I also asked him to help us manage our time and run our household better. This was a prayer deep in my heart and what a gift it was to be able to express it.

God continued to unfold the answers to our prayer through the summer. With our first child came a lot of new experiences for us. We had survived the first eight months of parenthood together and it brought us closer in many ways. Things had stabilized the following spring and summer. They were better than before, so we thought it was an improvement. If you had asked us how things were going in our marriage, we would have said things were good, but we still had some blocks between us. It was good, but "fine" might be a more accurate word to use to describe our marriage, which for the moment we were very grateful for. The rest of the summer God answered my prayer, one day at a time, and prepared Carmen and me to accept and receive more of His help.

Later that fall I attended a weekend retreat at Guidance for a Better Life. During that retreat God more fully answered the prayers in my heart I had expressed in the spring. Through His Prophet Del Hall III, He helped me see what I truly wanted and gave me truth that helped us start living the marriage both Carmen and me wanted and that God wanted for us. He helped me see what I could not see and gave me the tools to help Carmen and me recreate our marriage and how we related to each other.

I left the retreat with hope that things could truly be better for us. That "fine" was not good enough and we both deserved better. I now realized loving each other was not enough. We had to learn how to express our love daily and learn how to truly live with each other. That evening when I arrived home I expressed to Carmen that I wanted to live. I truly wanted us to live; truly live and have an abundant marriage, the marriage we both want and the marriage God wants for us. I wanted to start living differently than we had been living, and that "fine" was not good enough and we both deserved better. Expressing this desire and God's Divine Grace is what started the real change in our marriage. This was much better than four years of wishing and hoping things would get better. We were going to have to do something different than we had done in the past.

Learning to Clearly Communicate

I came into the marriage with insecurities I picked up along the way. These insecurities caused all kinds of arguments. When you feel good about yourself, you don't need your spouse to keep reassuring you and giving you feedback on how you and the marriage are doing every five minutes. I realize now I don't need to keep seeking Carmen's approval. This manifested in our marriage as a trap we kept falling into. Instead of expressing our love to each other, we often felt like the other person was supposed make us feel good. It was very confusing for both of us to figure out when the other needed a vote of confidence or how the other wanted us to be in the moment. We were, in a sense, taking turns demanding the other to guess what was on our mind. Both of us wanted to be reassured and we expected the other to read minds. We thought the other should just know. When our demands were not met we unconsciously withheld our love from each other. I didn't make a conscious choice to withhold my love from Carmen, but that is what often happened. My automatic response when things heated up was to put up a wall and shelter in place. When I became defensive or withdrawn it slowed the love flowing between us. When Carmen did not read my mind or vice versa, we would get upset and start a downward spiral. Then when we finally hit bottom I couldn't remember how we got there. After a fight it took time to feel safe to open back up.

Expecting Carmen to read my mind is not only unfair but it is also unrealistic. I didn't recognize this until Prophet pointed it out to me. This was a big source of our problem. Now that we could name it and recognize it we could do something positive. Until this point our needs went unmet and unexpressed many times. I am not a mind reader and no longer expect Carmen to be one. I am learning to ask Carmen for what I need from her and learning to express myself more clearly. This has improved things greatly for us. One thing I had to do was get over feeling guilty or uncomfortable about asking Carmen to give me what I need. Now that we are learning to communicate and express ourselves better we are also beginning to make more room for us to be ourselves. I am not spending as much time trying to figure out how I think she wants me to be. I'm learning to communicate more clearly and say what is on my mind and in my heart.

Learning How to Express Love

Carmen and me have always loved each other. It is something that has not waned, but we were not very good at expressing that love. More specifically we were not expressing our love in a way the other was receptive to receive it. Love not only needs to be given, but it also needs to be received by our spouse. If the love is there inside us but not expressed, or it is expressed but not received, it is not given a chance to do its work. Once we started learning to express love better we quickly noticed it also had to be received. Love expressed has to have somewhere to go to be of real value.

While writing this book we have discovered

that there seems to be a connection to how we view ourselves and how receptive we are to love from our spouse. The better and more secure one feels, it appears the more receptive to love one is. This also goes for our relationship with God. The more secure and the better we feel about ourselves in a balanced healthy way, the more receptive we are to receiving God's Love. Becoming receptive to God's Love and truth has made a huge difference in our lives. The more we can give and receive love with our spouse, the more we can give and receive God's Love in our lives. The more love and truth we can accept from God the more love we can experience with and accept from our spouse. The two marriages help nourish, grow, and support each other.

During the November retreat Del had recommended Carmen and I read a book called The Five Love Languages by Dr. Gary Chapman. There are of course more than five, but reading this book was a real blessing. It helped me start understanding how to express love better, and how to express it in a way Carmen can accept it.

Something else occurred after I followed this guidance from Del. As I read this book, God began making changes in the way I thought. Up to this point, I primarily expressed love to Carmen by telling her I loved her. I found it odd that she needed reassurance that I loved her, even though I said it daily. For some reason she did not believe me and it was not enough. I genuinely wanted Carmen to feel the love I had for her, but I began to realize this may mean I needed to express my love in new and uncomfortable ways.

I also started to develop new habits. One habit I had in our relationship was after an argument I would explain to Carmen why I had reacted a certain way. If she would have put something in a different way she would have gotten a different response. I thought this was sharing how I felt. It all seemed very logical to me. Cause and effect, very simple, and I made great effort to help her understand where I was coming from. This was usually during or after an apology and I genuinely believed it. In my mind it made perfect sense to me.

God had to heal my brain if Carmen and I were going to have a chance at growing in abundance. It came to the point where I had to ask myself the question: Did I want to be right or did I want to express love to my wife? This realization made quite a shift in my thoughts and eventually my actions. What was really more important to me? Did I want to put loving my wife first above loving my self? This realization began making changes in my other actions. We all have a choice and God has given me a chance to do something about it. With this came a second lesson for me. Was I going to continue to express my love the way I was comfortable, or was I going to figure out Carmen's primary love language? Was I going to learn my spouse's love language, no matter how foreign it seemed to me? Yes, I was going to learn how to express love the way she could receive it best. This is, in a way, putting her first above what I was comfortable doing, above what I was used to doing. Turns out, we discovered she likes to spend quality time together and have quality conversations where I express my thoughts and feelings to her. This fills her with love better than my telling her she is loved daily, and is what I needed to hear. We can learn to become receptive to our spouse and learn how we each give and receive love most fluently.

Sharing my thoughts and feelings with her literally terrified me; it was not something I grew up doing. It is one of the things she needs to feel loved by me, so I made a conscious choice to put the importance of her feeling loved higher than my deep embedded fears and my comfort level. I'm learning to express my feelings better. It's one of those things I just never learned growing up. I had to change some things if this was going to work.

As I began to learn to recognize and express my feelings more, I also began to give Carmen and myself the freedom to be upset, angry or whatever, and accepted that her mood may not have anything to do with me. This new attitude gave us some breathing room. It allowed us to be okay with being angry or having whatever emotion we might be experiencing at the time. We just needed to learn to express our feelings and emotions in a loving way. For the first time in my life it was okay to be angry. Instead of covering things up or ignoring them and hoping they would go away, we began to talk about them. We began to listen to each other without getting defensive and began to work some things out. We can now have a conversation and talk about issues. Once we began talking again and actually communicating, things began to turn around for us. We are actually both learning to zip it and let the other talk, without getting defensive. I've realized her mood may or may not have anything to do with me. If it has something to do with me I am now able to listen to what is bothering her. If it is about me she will communicate it. This eased things up for both of us. If I have something going on I am working through, I simply tell Carmen, "I am upset and it has nothing to do with you." She gets it and no longer has to wonder if I am mad at her, and doesn't let me being upset ruin her evening. This new attitude is giving Carmen more freedom to be herself, and is giving me more freedom too.

Along with this came another gift. One of the greatest things I began doing was to stop trying to fix whatever was going on in Carmen's life and instead just listen to her and let her express herself. I thought if she was upset about something, and she was talking to me about it, she wanted me to share one of my bright ideas to help her resolve the situation. It took some discipline on my part to zip it because I genuinely want to help her, but doing this has paid great dividends in our marriage. It has paid out in peace, joy, and freedom for both of us. Turns out if she wants my advice she will actually ask me. Many times she just wants to express herself. I have also learned when she does ask me for advice, to ask the inner Prophet what would help Carmen best and for the wisdom to know when to share it and when to keep it to myself.

A Beautiful New Opportunity

We have been given the opportunity to break family cycles that have existed for generations. We are grateful for this opportunity and are now passing on a new example to our one year old daughter. We want to teach our daughter by example how to express the love and divinity inside her, as well as how to express her emotions, thoughts, and feelings in a healthy and productive way. For love to do its work in a marriage it must be expressed and received. Our actions are some of the most influential teachers. Thank you Prophet, for blessing our marriage and giving us renewed hope and a chance to live the marriage of our dreams. Thank you God for sending your Prophet to help us learn to express and accept love better, live this life more abundantly, for guiding us home to you, and bringing Heaven to Earth in our daily lives. God, thank you for loving us, we love you.

Written by Mark Snodgrass

5

Blessed by Prophet
Paul's Story

Cathy and I were two independent individuals who came together in marriage later in our lives. For the first few years together, in some ways we lived separate lives under the same roof. As each of us grew closer to God by putting God first in our lives, God blessed us with the joy of gradually growing closer to each other in many new and different ways. We have come so far in this process that we are sold on it and want to share the joy of some of our lessons with you.

My Early Years

I was the second of four sons born into a loving Christian home. My father was a Baptist minister and my mother was an elementary school teacher. I had a happy childhood, did well in school, played sports, and was active in the church. Overall I was not too much of an embarrassment for my parents, except that as a teenager I wore my hair long, which was different. I am so grateful for my mother and father and the lessons in patience and responsibility they taught me.

For the first forty or so years of my life however, the decisions I made on what to do were largely based on what I thought other people wanted me to do. I had no real concept of who I was or what I really wanted in life. By outward appearances my life and first marriage were ideal. We had a nice house, good careers, and were active in church, but things were not as ideal as they seemed. Because of my vanity and self-indulgence, my apparently ideal marriage ended in divorce. It is amazing that it lasted as long as it did; twenty-two years. Soon after that, I was fed up with the career I had fallen into early in life and wanted out of that too; resigning after twenty-three years.

This was the classic mid-life crisis. Looking back though, I see it was actually the beginning of my mid-life awakening. Rather than living a life of doing what I thought others wanted me to do, I began to search for who I really was, wanting to live a life solely around following my own heart.

As humans often do, I swung the pendulum too far the other way, becoming very self-centered and not considering what I could be doing for others. Looking back now, I see clearly that I was allowing my vanity to take over my life. At the time however, I was not even aware of my vanity. I just wanted to be free to do what I wanted to do.

By the Grace of God, this was precisely the time in my life when I learned about Guidance for a Better Life, and Del Hall III became my spiritual teacher. Without the loving correction and Divine healings that came to me through this Prophet of God, my life would no doubt have descended to the depths of disaster. Looking back I see clearly how well God was preparing me for what was to come.

Healings

Many healings start as an insight of truth about ourselves that we were not aware of. How do we get that insight? We have to want the truth about ourselves, and we have to surrender our attachments to whatever is holding us back. For me, I had an out of control vanity and a lust for self-indulgence. These fed each other and held me back from growing closer to God.

Do you think I figured these things out for myself? No way! On my own I did not have a clue. Without the Grace of God through Del's teaching and guidance, these passions would still have me by the throat. I was living my life day-to-day completely blind to these barriers. They were revealed to me incrementally, in small portions, over time in perfect sequence. In just the right sized steps, I was allowed to see them clearly for what they were. I was allowed to experience how painfully harmful they really were. Then, when I no longer needed that lesson, by the Grace of God, through direct experience with the Light and Sound of God, each barrier was removed. This process is continuing. There is always more when it comes to spiritual growth.

One of the first steps in this process was when Del taught me HU. I began to sing this ancient name for God as a love song to God. Singing HU tunes us in to the "God channel" so to speak, and raises us up so we begin to see things about our life from a higher perspective. It is like when you cannot see the forest for the trees, climbing a tree gives you a wider view of where you are and how your current situation fits into the surrounding lay of the land. Rising in a hot air balloon can reveal even more, showing what is beyond the hills and valleys. This is sort of a metaphor for traveling as Soul, but we all need a guide.

None of us are equipped to travel in this way alone. God always has an inner guide, a Prophet of the times on Earth to help us. The Prophet is a living person who can teach in the outer physical world as well as on the inner, teaching us in dreams and visions where he takes us safely into God's inner worlds to learn exactly what we need for the next step in our spiritual unfolding. This is the Comforter, the incarnation of the Holy Spirit that Jesus spoke of in the Book of John.

About sixteen years ago, Del Hall III personally introduced me to the man who was God's chosen Prophet at that time. I never met him in the physical, only on the inner through real spiritual experiences. I remember the first time he appeared to me without spoken words and beckoned me to follow him, and I did. For fourteen years I learned from him on the outer by reading books he had written and watching videos of his talks. I learned from him so much more on the inner through dreams he gave me while sleeping, through awake dreams, through "coincidences" in my life, and through many inner experiences with the Light and Sound of God. These were adventures he took me on while I was in contemplation with him.

By far the most important thing Del ever taught me was to cultivate my relationship with God's chosen Prophet of the times. I instinctively knew this was essential because I already had a close inner relationship with Jesus, the true, literal Son of God, my Lord and Savior. Jesus was clearly pointing me to the one who is alive on Earth now, whom Jesus himself asked the Heavenly Father to send to us. Del Hall III became God's chosen Prophet of the times on October 22, 2012. Through many profound spiritual experiences, God has revealed this to me beyond any shadow of doubt.

Putting God First

I have learned through experience that a true love relationship between two people on Earth is actually a love triangle, with God at the top of the triangle, and the two partners at the two lower corners. As each of us individually grows closer to God, we become closer to each other. By putting God first in our lives, our earthly relationships become better and better.

"Seek ye first the kingdom of God and His righteousness, and all these things shall be added unto you." Matthew 6:33 KJV

More Reverence for God, for Cathy, and for Myself

I was sitting quietly with the group of students at a spiritual retreat at Guidance for a Better Life thinking how grateful I was to be there, and this opened my heart wide. God speaks to us through an open heart. Gratitude opens the heart. Del Hall III began guiding us in a sacred contemplation. We closed our eyes and began singing HU, a love song to God. We were all singing together, what a beautiful sound! After a few minutes with my physical eyes closed, something began to appear in front of me. It was the radiant form of a man whose face I recognized as God's Prophet of the times.

He lovingly lifted me up onto an ethereal sandy beach, at the edge of a beautiful ocean. He and I were on our knees with our heads bowed in reverence. I thanked my spiritual guide for bringing me here. I experienced waves of overwhelming love, peace, a deep feeling of reverence for God, and appreciation for this sacred experience with the Divine. I slowly looked up and God's Ocean was completely calm, like a mirror. I leaned forward to look into the water and saw a reflection of myself. What I saw has changed my life. Expecting to see my face with skin, eyes, nose, mouth, ears, instead what I saw was a bright shining ball of light vibrating with the Sound of God. I was seeing the real me for the first time. I am Soul!

This experience started a process of growing reverence for myself as a child of God. I felt overwhelming love and a calm peace that relaxed me to my very core. This feeling of God's Love and peace was so deep that I am not able to adequately describe it with words. I knew this is my eternal home.

Then my perspective turned to see other precious Souls also present on the beach. They too were bright, beautiful balls of light that were individualized. I could tell who each one was. My wife Cathy was there! I saw her as a beautiful ball of Light and Sound vibration. My love and appreciation for her became so intense that it changed how I relate to her.

After this experience I was aware of being

back inside my body, but I knew this body was not the real me. It is only the outer covering I wear like a suit in order to be able to function and interact in this physical universe. When I shared this amazing experience with the others in the group, Del explained that as Soul, we are made of the same raw material as the Voice of God, which is God's Light and Sound. No, I was not God. That is impossible. But God created me in His own image, with Divine attributes such as love, peace, joy, wisdom, and much more. These are what I was being lovingly shown in this sacred up-close and personal experience. This is what it really means to be made in the image of God. The experience was an amazing gift.

Over the years I have been given many inner experiences in God's Heavens. Each visit has cleansed, healed, strengthened, and nourished me. With each successive experience I was enabled to identify more and more with myself as Soul rather than as this physical body.

The same applies to how I see others, which changes how I relate to them. At work, seeing my boss and fellow workers as Soul has helped me immensely. At home it makes our marriage so much sweeter. My dear wife Cathy is not that redheaded body. She is Soul! I appreciate, respect, and cherish her so much more now, having experienced repeatedly who she really is. I was shown the real Cathy, that sacred bright shining ball of God's Light and Sound with whom I have been given the privilege of spending this lifetime! This has given me a new attitude of reverence for her, and gratitude for this wondrous gift from God in my life.

Separate Laundry and Caring for Mom

When Cathy and I got married on June 21, 2003, I had been divorced from my first marriage and living alone for six years. Cathy had been divorced from her first marriage and living alone for over twenty years. One of the things about living alone is you become accustomed to doing things your own way. One of these things was laundry.

I separated my clothes into two piles. Whites went into one pile, and everything else went into the other pile. The whites got hot water wash and warm water rinse in the regular cycle. The rest got warm water wash and cold rinse in the permanent press cycle. Everything went into the dryer together on the permanent press cycle.

Cathy's laundry was a bit more complex. The two pile system was not sufficient. She had some clothes that could only be washed in cold water, some that needed to be turned inside out before washing, and some that needed the delicate cycle. Then the dryer settings were different for different clothing items, and some could not be dried in the dryer at all but needed to be hung up to dry. I had a difficult time distinguishing these nuances so we fell into the habit of each doing our own laundry. It seemed to work for us at the time. We did this for several years. This may seem like an okay arrangement, but it was an indication of how we related to each other in many other areas of our lives. *We were self-centered.*

For my own part, I felt that if two piles were good enough for my own laundry, then two piles should be sufficient for hers too. Keep it simple. Get the task done. What does this indicate about my reverence for Cathy? It was actually a symptom of the larger defect in our togetherness. It affected everything in our marriage, not just the laundry. If I really loved and respected my wife, perhaps I would have wanted to learn those nuances about her laundry, and would have wanted to make the time and effort to know how she wanted her laundry done. If I was lazy about learning her laundry wishes, what else about her was I too lazy to learn?

Then something changed in our lives that helped us turn our focus away from ourselves. My mother developed dementia and needed to have more help with her living arrangements. Dad had passed away thirty years earlier. Mom moved into a retirement community one mile from our house. This was a perfect arrangement, allowing me to stop by her new apartment two to three days per week to check on her. I took her shopping for groceries, made sure she was getting her meals and taking her medications, arranged for laundry service, and whatever else she needed. I felt blessed to have this precious time with her and realized that my time was not my own anymore. Prophet had helped prepare me for this over the years and I saw the Hand of God in the whole arrangement.

It was such a joy to give of my time and energy to her. Mom had given so much of herself for my three brothers and me when we were children, and now it was my opportunity to give back and help her. I did not expect Cathy to disrupt her daily routine but she did graciously pitch in to help. Mom just loved it when Cathy would come with me to play her favorite game,

Scrabble. We spent many hours laughing and joking and learning new words.

One day I came home from one of my visits with Mom and found Cathy had done something unusual for me. She had done my laundry! What a blessing this was! It touched me deeply and I was brought to tears of gratitude and relief. She had recently experienced a weeklong retreat at Guidance for a Better Life and she was becoming a more giving person.

I noticed Cathy began doing more nice things for me, and she began reaching out to help the widow who lives alone across the street from us. She was also mending her relationship with one of her sisters whom she had drifted apart from and began to initiate more contact with both of her sisters and her stepmother. It was obvious that she was also experiencing less stress and more joy in her life. As she grew in her ability to give and receive love, my love for her grew.

God also healed me directly through His Prophet. Cathy and I discovered something. As we focused our time and energy on helping Mom and others, we experienced more joy and love ourselves. Del has taught us that service is its own reward and we were now experiencing this first hand.

As Mom's dementia progressed, she needed

more and more help. I was spending more and more time helping as her needs increased. Then she was diagnosed with cancer. She needed radiation treatment five days per week and chemotherapy one day per week. Each weekday for eight weeks, I would get off work, pick her up and go for a ride to the hospital for these treatments. With Prophet's inner guidance always with me, we found home health nurses to come into her apartment and help her each day. I arranged for a companion to take her to her treatment one day per week. Cathy helped too, which gave me a welcomed break.

After the eight weeks of cancer treatments, Mom's pain and disfigurement were held in check but the cancer had spread into her lungs. This was a very aggressive form of cancer called angiosarcoma. Mom's prognosis was grim, and the doctors discontinued her treatments and placed her into palliative care to keep her comfortable. They suggested I let family members know that it could be only a matter of days now, so I did. All my brothers came to see her and she was happy we were all together.

Cathy especially helped me more and more, and as we both gave more of ourselves for Mom, we gave more of ourselves for each other too. Through this process, God was bringing Cathy and me closer together. I now see this was God's plan. Mom must have known too, because she suddenly began to get better and lived another three months! That extra blessed time was sweet. It gave Cathy and me that much more opportunity to grow closer to God and to each other as we relied on Prophet for inner strength and guidance. Thank you Mom! Thank you God!

After Mom went home to Heaven, I found myself wanting to give more of myself to Cathy. One way was to learn all the nuances of doing her laundry the way she likes it done. Why not just let her continue to do hers in her detailed way, and let me do mine in the simple way? Well, Prophet has taught us that love is to be demonstrated. I wanted to demonstrate to her that I cherish her and respect her desires for taking care of her fine clothing.

When I did finally begin that process, I found that I actually began to appreciate her clothes more. I saw the value in them, and I began to see more value in Cathy's keen eye for detail, which is something I have begun to admire and want to emulate. It has helped me appreciate my wife more! Besides, who knows, some day Cathy may need to be spending many hours caring for her own stepmother, and I could be a lot more useful to her as a loving husband whom she could trust to help out by doing her laundry the way she prefers.

I discovered that as I demonstrated more love for Cathy in this and other ways, my love for her grew. Now, sometimes she does the laundry and sometimes I do. Whenever it needs to get done, it gets done. Life is sweet. Thank you Prophet!

Separate Bank Accounts

As each of our relationships with God grew through sacred experiences with the Divine, we began to see material things differently. All things in this material world began fading into relative insignificance compared to the riches of spiritual reality. It all belongs to God.

Our bodies, our material possessions, our financial income, are all His, entrusted to us for safekeeping during each lifetime. As I began to grow in this truth, my attachments to money and material things began to melt away. At the same time, I began to appreciate them more as blessings from God. Being less attached to material things helps us live happier lives because if something is taken away from us, we are not devastated by the loss. By recognizing these as blessings from God, I began to ask myself what is the best use of my time and money, making conscious choices with Prophet's help. How well I take care of them according to God's will is a demonstration of my love and appreciation.

For several years Cathy and I had separate bank accounts. We kept a monthly ledger sheet of who paid each bill. Then we divided each expense fifty/fifty and settled up at the end of the month by one of us writing a check to the other to balance the ledger. We spent a lot of time logging each transaction, keeping receipts, and painstakingly dividing expenses evenly.

Something changed within us as God brought us closer together. As we became less attached to, and more appreciative of the finances entrusted to us, Prophet helped us become more generous and more frugal at the same time. Our trust in God has grown as He provides all we need and then some. Our trust in each other also grew and we wanted to share more of ourselves with each other, including the earnings God has entrusted to us. So we went to the banks together and changed our accounts to joint accounts. We began to pool our resources and totally abandoned the monthly ledger system. Wow, what a relief! What a joy it is to be free of that burden. There is a deep appreciation and trust for each other that has blossomed from this. It was another important step in our marriage that eliminated a major headache and has made our life together that much sweeter.

Abundant Life

"I am come that they might have life, and that they might have it more abundantly." John 10:10 KJV

What I have learned from Del is that the abundant life is not about doing everything I thought others wanted me to do, nor is it about doing everything my own lower human desires want to do. Rather, the abundant life is about identifying with myself as Soul, a child of God, and being in a close, true love relationship with the God of ultimate creation through His indwelling Spirit, personified as God's chosen Prophet of the times. This is precisely what Jesus taught. His teachings have come alive for me in ways that my human mind could never have understood even with lifetimes of going to church. The difference has been true sacred experiences with the Divine, guided by the loving, all-knowing Prophet, who knows me better than I know myself, and who sees all things that I am not seeing about myself.

My essential role in manifesting the blessings of abundant living is to nurture this relationship in part, through daily spiritual food. Without it we become spiritually malnourished. Spiritual strength is developed through direct experiences with the Love of God. Some of the ways I stay nourished are by singing HU, spending time in prayer and contemplation with the Prophet, experiencing the Light and Sound of God, studying the scriptures, studying the dreams I am given, appreciating Prophet's presence, and seeing God's Hand in the events of daily life. The real banquets of spiritual food are the retreats we regularly attend at Guidance for a Better Life!

With love for the true teachings of God.

Written by Paul Harvey Sandman

6

Blessed by Prophet
Cathy's Story

Childhood

My memories of early childhood are of a happy family. We had the "traditional" family in the late 1950s and 60s: my dad worked outside the home, and my mom stayed home and took care of three daughters who were about four years apart in age from the oldest to the youngest. I remember happy Christmases, Easter Sundays, and other precious times together as a family. I remember there being music in our home. My dad and mom would sit at the piano together to play songs and sing, and get up and dance together doing the Jitterbug. I remember all of us laughing together. I remember going to church sometimes and attending Vacation Bible School when I was about four years old. I remember feeling safe, secure, and carefree in the neighborhoods we lived in, being able to leave home for hours at a time and ride our bikes safely throughout our neighborhood, and playing softball on the vacant corner lot down the street. We never had to worry whether some evil person was going to try to kidnap us. Mom would call us back home for lunch and dinner by ringing a bell that was loud enough for us to hear just about anywhere in our neighborhood. What sweet memories.

My parents' marriage started falling apart when I was ten or eleven years old, and it was not long afterward that they separated and eventually divorced. Life for my sisters and me changed drastically after that. During that time divorce was almost unheard of. I do not remember any of my friends or schoolmates having experienced it. There was probably a stigma about us that I was not aware of at the time. We lived with my mom for a few years, seeing my dad on weekends and going on vacations with him. Mom loved us very much but had some personal problems. She left, and my dad took full custody of my two sisters and me. I was not consciously aware of it at the time, but I now know that God was blessing all of us, including Mom, by my dad accepting the responsibility with love of taking care and custody of three teenaged daughters. Dad got married several years later to a wonderful woman who became our stepmother. She was sixteen years younger than Dad and had no children, so she stepped into a ready-made family and with love provided guidance and nurturing to all of us. She was a blessing from God for all of us.

Teen Years

During my teenage years I attended a Baptist church with friends I knew at school. I do not remember much about it other than their friendship and love, and sharing fun wholesome times together. Reflecting on that time as an adult I know in my heart that God was always with me, guiding and directing me out of harm's way, and protecting me; as it would have been easy for an impressionable young girl to "fall into the wrong group" and do things that would have harmed me or I would have regretted.

When I was in the ninth grade and fifteen years old I met a guy, whom I will call John, one day while I was at a local shopping center. I knew he went to my junior high school but had never really met him or talked with him. We chatted for a few minutes. I immediately felt a connection with him and I could tell he felt it too. We started encountering each other in the hallways between classes, greeting each other with a friendly "hello." Brief hellos turned into conversations and getting to know each other. He asked me to be his partner in a school intramural egg toss contest. We ended up winning it! Our friendship grew. He belonged to a church with different beliefs than any church I was familiar with, and he was deeply entrenched in those beliefs and committed to his religion. He was a very nice, friendly, wholesome guy with a good sense of humor and was fun to be with. We started hanging out, playing tennis, riding bicycles, taking walks, and attending school functions together. We even had part-time jobs at the same local restaurant. We had a great friendship and in essence we were dating.

John told me that his parents liked me and thought I was a nice person, but they told him he and I could not date because I did not belong to their church or have the same beliefs they have. Their beliefs were so different that it would have caused problems, and they did not believe in dating, or marriage outside of their religion. My friendship with him and growing love for him were so strong that with my dad's permission I decided to go to his church. I attended his church weekly, a Bible study weekly, and annual out-of-state conventions with his family. I started feeling like I was drifting away from my family and feeling inner conflict and sadness because John's religion did not celebrate birthdays or holidays, which were always so important to my family and to me personally. I ended up joining the church and was baptized into that religion. My relationship with John continued throughout all of high school. We spent a lot of time together. Looking back I know my heart really was not in the religion. I loved John so much, felt secure with him, and wanted to be with him. I realized later in life that dating one guy steadily throughout high school protected me from getting involved in some not-so-wholesome activities that some of my classmates were experimenting with and with some not-so-wholesome people. I am really grateful to God for His protection.

My First Marriage

I graduated high school, started a full-time job, and got married to John all within six months at eighteen years old. John was a very nice, kind, gentle Soul. We got along well and were best friends. The main reason we divorced was because of his religious beliefs that I eventually realized I could no longer live with. I felt sad, oppressed and imprisoned, and had lost some of the deep connection I felt with my family and lost a lot of myself. I did not know who I was. I felt sad because I really liked John and loved him, but I knew in my heart I could not continue in the marriage. It was not fair to either of us to try to make it work since I could no longer be in that religion. My feelings about the religion and my growing inactivity in attending church services and Bible studies with him were putting a wedge between us. At my request, after about four years of marriage, John and I divorced. We had no children. He moved out of state and we kept in touch from time to time, until he told me he was going to get married. We knew it would not be appropriate for us to continue to stay in touch, so we said good-bye and wished each other well. It was a blessing for both of us that we divorced. He was able to marry and share life with someone who had a heart for the religion that was so much a part of him and his life.

Single Adult

I spent the next twenty-three years as a single person. I was blessed and grateful to have a well-paying job right out of high school and be able to buy a house at the age of twenty-three. I learned to be self-sufficient. I was blessed to receive a lot of help from my loving dad and stepmom, and a wonderful neighbor who lived across the street. After the divorce I felt so free and liberated. I experienced many new adventures: whitewater rafting, water-skiing, snow-skiing, taking trips, and attending social events and concerts with friends. In my mid-thirties I joined a singles group at a prominent Baptist church in the city and within a few years was baptized. I developed close friendships. I traveled internationally for the first time in my life to Kenya and Tanzania in Africa with a small group of friends from church on a two-week mission trip to teach Vacation Bible School to young children. We even went on a safari. What a blessed and life-changing experience that entire trip was! I also traveled on an adventurous social trip to Reykjavík, Iceland with a few friends from church. During those years I dated several guys, always in search of "the one." Whenever I met a guy and became interested in him I would wonder, "Is he my future husband?" I was looking for love but not sure what I was looking for as I still was not really sure who I was.

I dated a man from work whom I will call Dean, who was separated from his wife. I knew in my mind and heart that dating a man who was separated was not a wise thing to do but felt a strong connection with him and dated him anyway. It was a roller coaster ride with many ups and downs and heartaches, but I continued to see him hoping that we would eventually be together in a permanent relationship. Knowing how lost and confused he felt (and in retrospect I realize I was led by God), I suggested he look into the Divorce Recovery Program sponsored by the Baptist church I attended, hoping it would help him. He signed up for the program. We eventually parted ways, but during the course of our dating I went with Dean to a social gathering of a small group in the Divorce Recovery Program at a local restaurant, Rare Old Times in March of 2000. There I met a very nice guy Paul (his real name!). He was involved in the same Divorce Recovery Program that Dean was. Paul had been divorced for a couple of years. I had no interest in him as my heart was still with Dean, even though our relationship was turbulent, unsteady, and falling apart. A couple of days later Paul called Dean and asked if he and I were dating. Dean said, "Well sort of," to which Paul replied, "Well okay, then I won't ask her to go out."

Dean and I continued to see each other for a little while longer. I would see Paul when I attended Music Night gatherings with Dean. Music Night was a social gathering held once a month at the homes of the same Divorce Recovery friends that I had met at Rare Old Times. Paul and I had a shared interest in music as both of us played the guitar, sang, and loved John Denver's music. Having this connection with Paul and seeing him once a month provided a way for us to get to know each other gradually, without expectations of possibly dating. He even hosted a cookout and Music Night at his home which Dean and I attended.

Having a relationship with Dean was not wise because of his marital status and all the repercussions that entailed, but I feel it was meant to be because it is through him that I met Paul. I am grateful to the Divine for the connection that led me to meeting Paul, who in turn brought me to Guidance for a Better Life, all of which changed my life.

Dean and I broke up within a few months. I

was still somewhat in contact with him because we worked in the same office. Through Dean, I found out that Paul was experiencing problems with his job. He had been with his State job for about twenty-three years and was feeling stressed and burned out with the bureaucratic world. He decided to take a five-week vacation and drive across country alone in hopes he would then be able to make a decision whether to stay with his job until he could retire or resign. When Paul returned home from his travels near the end of July of 2000, he decided to quit his job. I found out that Paul went to Guidance for a Better Life to be an intern from late summer through that autumn. The Guidance for a Better Life retreat center was established in 1990 by Del Hall, teacher and true Prophet of God, and his wife Lynne. They offer spiritual retreats and classes taught by Del and his son that help Souls find their way home to God. An intern lives in a small, one-room, comfortable cabin on the retreat center property and is provided with the necessities of daily living. The intern helps Del and Lynne prepare the school building for students to attend retreats, and helps in other ways such as mowing grass, clearing walking trails, doing some planting, feeding their goats, running errands, etc. It is a blessed privilege to spend time on retreat center property and be of service to Del and Lynne.

Visit to Guidance for a Better Life

Around that same time I too was experiencing similar problems at my career job with the local telephone company where I had worked for twenty-five years. It had become very stressful for me. The company was rapidly changing and expanding, and was therefore experiencing major growing pains. I was feeling constant anxiety and it was affecting my health. I was having chest pains and feeling an increasing loss of joy and an onset of depression. I could see no improvement no matter how I tried to have a positive attitude and tried harder to comply with the changes and growth of the company. I was facing a difficult decision of quitting my job with a company I could retire from in five years at age forty-eight, having the security of retirement and health insurance benefits for the rest of my life.

I felt a nudge that I later knew was from Prophet to contact Paul and talk with him about his experiences with his job, his decision to quit, and where he planned to go from there, if indeed he had plans. A phone call to Paul at Guidance for a Better Life led to an invitation from him, with gracious permission from Del and Lynne, to visit him at the retreat center for a weekend. What an amazing blessing it was to be on the retreat center property, to be in the presence of Del and Lynne, and to spend time with Paul talking with him! I felt peace, love, tranquility, and joy as soon as I arrived on retreat center property. I felt welcomed by Del and Lynne. I relaxed and felt none of the anxiety of my stressful situation back home two hours away. I felt no pressure of the possibility of Paul being someone I might become romantically involved with, as I did not want a romantic relationship with anyone at that time in my life. He felt the same way. Therefore, we felt the freedom of sharing our feelings and having open-hearted discussions, and we became friends. I really enjoyed our time together. We took walks together, fed the goats, and led them to the fields to graze. Paul gave me a guided tour of the property showing me the beautiful pond, the shelters where students attending retreats slept, the walking trails, etc. I felt I was on holy ground.

After I left we stayed in contact, and a few weeks later he invited me to come back to visit him at the retreat center, again with Del and

Lynne's blessing. We had a wonderful friendly visit together for the weekend. Our talks helped me immensely with the situation I was going through at work and helped with my ultimate decision about my job. I know that throughout our time together we were being guided by Prophet.

While visiting Paul the second time I felt more comfortable with him and started to consider the possibility of developing a closer relationship with him, but suppressed my feelings, thinking it was still too soon for me to become involved with him or anyone romantically. During that visit he shared with me that he planned to go back out west to visit a lady he met and had developed an interest in during his five-week cross country travels that summer. I felt a pang in my heart. I realized I did not want him to go out west, but knew I could not ask him not to go. I surrendered the feelings and let go of the possibility of a relationship with him, knowing I was still not ready for one (or by now trying to convince myself of that). By going out west Paul would be shortening his internship by several weeks and leaving soon.

A couple weeks later on a Monday morning I awoke at the normal time to get up and get ready for work. I could not get out of bed. I just lay there, feeling frozen. When I attempted to sit up in bed, it felt like a hand was gently placed on my heart, pushing me back down. I inwardly heard a voice softly say, "You're not going anywhere." I tried to sit up again and was gently pushed back down. I lay there feeling bewildered, wondering what I should do. I searched my heart trying to come up with an answer. Searching my heart was really a prayer to God for help. I called my supervisor's telephone number at work and left a voicemail message that I would not be coming to work that day but would see her at work the next day. Later that morning still lying in bed and still feeling a bit bewildered, the thought came to me to call Del and Lynne to see if I could step in for Paul and finish the last three weeks of his internship at Guidance for a Better Life. I felt this would give me an opportunity to really clear my head, receive guidance, and prepare me for the possibility of making a life-changing decision of quitting my job. Del and Lynne graciously blessed me with the opportunity to do just that when they said yes! They were an answer to my prayer. Little did I know at the time that Del, soon to become God's Prophet of our times, would also be the answer to my future prayers.

As far as my job went, I ended up on a

disability leave of absence due to work stress and how it was affecting my health and quality of life. I would have to go through testing and wait for test results to determine what my next course of action would be. This time off provided me the three weeks I needed to be the intern for Del and Lynne. God's perfect timing. What a blessing! Regarding Paul, he decided not to go out west because of feelings he was starting to have for me. I was so delighted and grateful! He visited me for a few days during the time I was the intern at the retreat center. Our time together was such a blessing in so many ways. Spending time together on that blessed holy ground gave us the opportunity to nurture our friendship and a budding relationship.

I am eternally grateful to Del and Lynne, for so many reasons, for allowing me the opportunity to be their intern. The many beautiful experiences I was blessed with as their intern were life changing. I experienced many things I had not previously experienced, such as: living in that comfortable one-room cabin where I felt at home, feeding their goats and taking them for walks to the fields to graze, assisting Lynne with the birth of baby goats and bringing one baby back to the cabin with me to sleep overnight, running errands, being blessed to live in that beautiful paradise, the blessing of being of service and helping them as needed. I was helping Del and Lynne in some ways, but I am the one who received help, guidance, love, and blessings from God by the privilege of being there and serving. My time as an intern at the retreat center is one of the most memorable times of my life. The most beautiful and life-changing blessing I received while there was when Del taught me to sing HU, a love song to God and an ancient name for God. I have looked back and re-appreciated that blessing many times, knowing that Prophet himself blessed me and personally taught me HU. Thank you, Prophet!

Courtship With Paul

After I returned home from my internship, Paul and I made a vow to one another to exclusively date each other. Thus began our romantic relationship, the foundation being our love for God and our love for and friendship with each other. We continued dating and getting to know each other. I was still on my leave of absence. I remained hopeful I would be able to stay with the company but in a different, less stressful job so I could finish my tenure and receive full benefits at retirement. Paul was working at a new job doing brick and stonework outdoors, something he loved to do and an answer to his prayer! He really enjoyed working outdoors. I realized how much I like to work outdoors, not in an office, because of the time I spent as an intern at Guidance for a Better Life.

After almost six months on disability (which I know was a gift from the Divine of what I needed at that time), I received a call from a representative of my company notifying me that I had to go back to work, to the job that had stressed me out so greatly. I then spoke with my manager who informed me that there was no other job available I was qualified for within the company. My choices were to go back to the same stressful corporate-world office which I heard had gotten worse stress-wise, or quit. So after getting over the initial shock and then asking God for help and guidance to know what was in my best interests, I was given clarity and I resigned. I knew I had no other choice and had faith in God that I would find another job with His guidance and doing my part.

I regularly looked at the job listings in our local newspaper. One day a job listing jumped out at me from the page, which I know was Prophet's guidance. It was totally different from my former corporate job. The job was for an interiorscape company that provided indoor tropical plants and plant maintenance service to commercial and residential clients and was family-owned. I applied for the job. When I went for the interview I was told the job for which I had applied in the operations department was no longer available, but there was another job available involving taking care of tropical plants at clients' locations. The responsibilities and duties involved being out and about during the workday, going from location to location, interacting with and providing customer service to clients, and caring for the plants. I would be outdoors at times throughout the day, not in a cubicle in an office environment. I was very much interested and said "Yes!" I was hired and have been with the same company for almost fourteen years. After a couple of years in that position, I was able to get the job for which I originally applied and received a promotion after several years. Prophet never forgets. He knew my heart and blessed me with the opportunity to work in the department for which I initially applied.

Paul and I continued to date and our friendship continued to grow, as did our love for each other. We both felt we would eventually get married and occasionally talked about it. We had no definite plans, as we wanted to take our time getting to know each other and be sure of our decision. Neither of us wanted to go through another divorce. One of the roadblocks was that we both had houses and neither of us wanted to move. I had been in my house about twenty-two years and lived close to my work. Paul had lived in his house for about five years and liked the convenience of the location and the layout of his house. My house was a small one-story house and not ideal for two adults with accumulated "stuff" to blend together two households. We let it go and surrendered it to God. Another consideration for me was the fact that I had lived alone for those twenty-two years and was now in my mid-forties. As much as I loved Paul, I did not know if I would ever be capable of sharing a home with someone.

Paul and I planned a vacation to go to the Grand Canyon and other nearby parks in that area of the country in the summer of 2002. Just a few weeks before our vacation, the hose on my washing machine in my kitchen burst while I was at work and therefore had all day to flood the inside of my home with several inches of water, making it uninhabitable. At first I was in a fog, incredulous at the sight, trying to process what I was seeing and experiencing. Literally within minutes, a knowingness came over me. This was a blessing! Prophet had provided us the solution to our dilemma of whose house to live in should we get married! The insurance company estimated it would take approximately three months to repair the damage and make my home livable again. They offered to put me in a hotel and pay the room rate for the entire time it took to complete the repairs. Paul graciously offered that I live in his home while the repairs were being made, rather than living in a hotel. Again I knew this was the answer from God to a personal dilemma of mine – to find out if I could share living space, a home, with him.

I moved in with Paul immediately and gradually moved in some of my belongings. I knew within a short time that living with him in his home was a blessing. It is one thing to stay the night at the other person's place and then be able to go back to your own home and your own space the next day. It is an entirely different experience to live full-time with someone. One really gets to know the other person well by sharing day-to-day living – meals, laundry, grocery shopping, expenses, and bathrooms! I immediately realized how pleasant, gracious, and easy to live with Paul was. My fears and worries dissolved. I felt at home and at peace, very loved, very blessed, and very grateful.

We kept our vacation plans to go out west. I had no idea what Paul was planning to do at the North Rim of the Grand Canyon. We were standing together at a fenced edge overlooking the beauty and grandeur of the canyons, amazed by the breath-taking views and scenery. I was thinking how I had no doubt that God was the creator of this place! As I gazed out at the beautiful expanse of the canyon I remarked, "It just goes on forever." Paul later shared that this was the cue he had been waiting for. He immediately dropped to one knee and said, "Just like our love for each other. Will you marry me?" It was so unexpected and I was so surprised that I immediately replied, "Are you serious?" Reassured by Paul of his sincerity, I answered, "Yes!" It was a sweet, humorous, and memorable moment that we have reminisced about and shared with others from time to time over the years. We both recognize that the timing and opportunity for that beautiful moment was planned and made possible by God.

Now a Married Couple

About a year later on June 21, 2003, Paul and I were married. The years have flown by. God has abundantly and lovingly blessed us throughout our marriage. Paul and I like each other and we love each other. He is my friend and confidant. We have had and continue to have a very loving, peaceful, abundantly blessed marriage. We laugh and have fun together. We pray and sing HU together. We are kind to each other and express gratitude to one another for the seemingly small things we do for each other. He continues to seat me at the dining table and open the car door for me. There have been only a few times throughout our relationship and marriage that we have raised our voices at each other in anger or disagreement. I know without a doubt that Prophet is helping us work through issues (also known as opportunities for growth) by teaching us spiritual tools we consistently use in life and in our marriage. Paul and I both regularly attend retreats together at Guidance for a Better Life where Del Hall, the Prophet of our times, teaches. In addition to teaching us spiritual tools to use in our marriage and in all areas of our lives, he has shown and helped Paul and me, individually, areas we can grow and have a happier, more abundant life. Prophet has so much wisdom, knows us better than we know ourselves, and knows exactly what we need, which enables him to see traits and habits in us that we do not recognize. Some traits and habits block us personally and can put a wedge in our relationship with our spouse, and most importantly in our relationship with Prophet. He loves us so much and wants to help us work through and be healed of those traits. We have to be open and receptive to his help and do our part. One example for me is selfishness.

Having been single and living alone for twenty-three years after my divorce, I had developed very selfish tendencies and brought them into our marriage. Although I loved Paul with all my heart and was grateful and happy to be married to him, I did not trust that our marriage would last. That attitude put a wedge between us that I was not conscious of. For years in some areas of our lives we lived like roommates, such as keeping our finances separate and even doing our own laundry. I felt that by keeping our finances separate we both had an "out" should our marriage not succeed. God has blessed me with many opportunities that have helped me get over myself and my selfish ways by serving others with love through Divine guidance.

Prophet, Betty Jo, and Healings

The most precious opportunity of serving with love I have been blessed with up to the time of this writing is when Paul's mom Betty Jo was diagnosed with a rare and aggressive form of cancer in the autumn of 2014. For three years prior to that time, Paul had been Betty Jo's primary caretaker, as her other three sons lived many hours away. She had been diagnosed with dementia and was in pretty good physical health, but she increasingly needed help with her daily affairs such as finances, grocery shopping, laundry service, and housekeeping. She resided in an independent living apartment about one mile from our home. Paul arranged help for his mom for most of her needs, and he shopped for her groceries. He spent time with her and took her places. At first I was selfish with my time and many times did not accompany Paul and Betty Jo, but over time my love for her grew and I desired to be with her and spend more time with her. This was a blessing to me by the grace and wisdom of the Divine. Almost every Sunday, we would all three have lunch or dinner together and then play a fun game of Scrabble! I know that Prophet was helping me realize how precious our time together was, that life is short, and no one but our Heavenly Father knows how long any of us have in our bodies on this Earth. I looked forward to visiting Betty Jo, sometimes going with Paul and sometimes by myself. I grew to cherish and treasure our time together. After Betty Jo was diagnosed with cancer, she was prescribed radiation and chemotherapy. For the first few weeks, Paul was taking Betty Jo to radiation treatments five days a week and hired a companion to take her to chemotherapy one day a week. It became my heart's desire to help Paul (and Betty Jo) by taking her to one radiation treatment a week. This time of year was the busiest time at my work, the Christmas season. Employees are understandably not allowed to take time off during the Christmas season, except under emergency situations. I prayed to Prophet for guidance and help and was led by him to ask my employer if I may please take the afternoon off one day a week to take my mother-in-law to radiation treatment. Prophet provided me the window of opportunity at just the right time to ask. When I asked my employer, explaining the situation, with compassion and understanding she graciously said, "Yes, of course." I was so grateful to her and to Prophet!

The time Betty Jo and I spent together was a blessing to me. Prophet and I together were helping her by serving her with love, and I too was being blessed. Her prognosis was not good, just a few weeks, but an amazing thing happened! Her health started to improve for a while. This was a blessing from God that provided opportunities to help me continue to grow out of my selfish tendencies and grow in serving others with love, serving my dear mother-in-law. During this time at a weekend retreat at Guidance for a Better Life, Prophet knew and shared with Paul and me that Betty Jo was given a choice by the Divine (on the inner). She could have chosen to pass away and leave her body shortly after her cancer diagnosis or stay alive in her body longer to help Paul and me grow by serving her, which also helped us in our marriage. Out of her deep love for both of us she chose to stay alive in her failing body, enduring treatments, pain, and declining health. What an amazing, beautiful gift of love she gave us! From that time until she passed on April 1, 2015, time spent with her and helping her were some of the most blessed, precious times I have experienced. I appreciate with all my heart the love and grace shown me by Prophet and Betty Jo and the choice she made to live longer to help me grow. Thanks be to God for this beautiful lesson and opportunities to continue to grow in service to others!

Bad Case of Procrastination

Another negative trait I had was a bad case of procrastination that affected me personally and in turn affected my marriage with Paul, as well as other areas of my life. I believe I had been carrying that undesirable and lethal-to-a-happy-life trait for many lifetimes. Procrastination is a cancer to a person and a marriage. It was a bad habit that in this lifetime I could trace back to my days as a student in school. In my marriage I was not keeping up with chores at home. I consistently put things off. So things piled up and snowballed to the point where I did not know where to begin. Paul would take up the slack for me and do my chores, which was so unfair to him. I started feeling weighed down, in a rut, tired, lethargic, and stressed. I got to the point where I felt I would never catch up. I was not aware how it was affecting my relationship with Paul and most importantly my relationship with Prophet. Procrastination was blocking me and affecting my ability to give and receive love. Prophet could see I had this trait and how it was affecting all areas of my life. At Guidance for a Better Life during a weeklong retreat I was invited to attend, he brought this truth out into the open with love to help me. It was a personal gift of love. It was a life changing, healing experience for me to learn this truth and how with Prophet's help and doing my part I could change. He helped me realize how my entire life was being negatively affected by procrastination. I know if he hadn't brought this to my attention and helped me work through it and grow through it, my marriage with Paul would not have survived. I received his lesson of love and truth, and his healing as a gift of love and a blessing.

In hopes that it might help someone reading this, I would like to share the prescription and the homework Prophet lovingly and graciously gave me during the retreat that is blessing me and helping me get over myself and work through procrastination: "Do one or two things every day for someone else, out of love, preferably without their knowing about it. Serve others with love." I gratefully accepted and am following this prescription from God daily. It is changing my life and the way I see and interact with others. It is making an amazingly positive difference in all areas of my life, especially my relationship with Prophet and my marriage with Paul. I ask Prophet for help in being aware of opportunities to serve, help, and show love to Paul and others every day, preferably anonymously.

Gratitude to Prophet

I am eternally grateful to Prophet for his love, insight, healing, and the gifts of love and truth he gave me during this retreat. He continues to bless me throughout every day. He loves us so much. He loves me so much. He always has our best interests at heart and wants us to have a better, happier, and more abundant life.

Looking back and reflecting on my life before I consciously became aware of the presence of Prophet with me, I can see the Hand of God throughout my life's experiences. Even through seemingly tough times I know Prophet has always been with me through everything that has happened in my life. Through every moment, through every decision, he has always guided me. He has protected me and has literally saved my life in some situations that I am fully aware of and some I am not aware of, but I just know. I may not have always made the most logical or wise choices, but each choice and decision I made has taught me valuable lessons. I recognize Prophet's love and protection through events and experiences I had before I was guided by him to come to Guidance for a Better Life. I can see that before he led me to the retreat center, he guided me to explore and open up to different spiritual paths and beliefs such as: karma, awareness of past lives, reincarnation, and being Soul versus having a Soul. This helped me to get outside the confines of the box of beliefs I had been in during my life in the traditional churches.

Prophet opened me up to consider a relationship with someone I may not have considered in the past. Paul is a loving, giving Soul. In past relationships I usually was the pursuer of men who were not available, either emotionally or relationally. My relationship with Paul started out differently. We started as friends first. I did not pursue him. At first, I had no interest in a relationship with him other than a friendship. He is a loving, gracious, thoughtful, generous, and giving Soul.

I know that if I had not been aware of and open to Prophet's love, truth, guidance, wisdom, help, peace, and teachings, I would not still be married to Paul. I would have gone through another divorce.

Spiritual Tools That Bless Our Marriage

There are so many spiritual tools and teachings I am blessed with by Prophet that are helping me as an individual and in my relationship with and marriage to Paul. If I had to choose one specific tool as the most important, it is that God is the foundation of our marriage. We each put God first in our individual lives and our spouse second. Putting God first and as the foundation of our marriage is benefiting us in so many ways. It is making our marriage richer, sweeter, more intimate, more peaceful, more fun, and helping us grow in our love for each other every day. Loving God and putting my relationship with Him first is teaching me what a true, loving relationship is. It is helping me appreciate Paul for who he is, to value and treasure him, respect him, be open honest and truthful with him and see him as Soul. It is helping me to learn on a deeper level how to give and receive love, and to serve my husband with love. Putting God first is also deepening my ability to have and show compassion for Paul. It is helping me be more accepting and appreciative of our differences. I am deeply grateful to be in a loving marriage and to be aware of and appreciate every blessing that God bestows on me personally and on our marriage every day.

I am grateful to Prophet for his love, truth, wisdom, guidance, teaching, grace, mercy, and constant presence with me. I am grateful to him for my personal growth, and the continuing growth of my love for Paul and my relationship and marriage with him. The love and strength of my sacred relationship with Prophet helps keep my marriage to Paul strong, solid, and sacred; resisting temptations and not allowing others into it. The "other side" can use subtle tactics to try to undermine a marriage, break it down, and destroy it. Daily spiritual exercises such as singing HU and spending focused quiet time daily with Prophet feed and nourish me, enabling me to stay strong in my relationship with him.

Through the years of attending classes and retreats at Guidance for a Better Life and developing the close, loving, sacred relationship

I have with Prophet, he is teaching me to be a better me, the real me as Soul - more loving, kind, considerate, compassionate, and thoughtful. With his help, I continue to grow in showing love, patience, mercy, grace, forgiveness, and understanding to Paul. Paul lovingly demonstrates these qualities to me. I love serving the Divine and becoming a more refined Instrument for God. I continue to learn how to lovingly demonstrate these qualities to Paul, as well as others, because Prophet teaches them to me by lovingly demonstrating them. These qualities bless me in every facet of my life.

Paul and I each spend quiet time alone with Prophet. Our marriage is enriched by also spending time together singing HU, a love song to God. We also make time to discuss and share with each other the teachings, truths, and blessings that Prophet lovingly gives us. This time together adds a dimension of spiritual intimacy to our relationship. I am deeply grateful to be a student of Prophet at Guidance for a Better Life and grateful that Paul and I share this path. I am learning many lessons through experiences and direct truth and love from Prophet that are enriching my life and my marriage beyond words. I know that God loves us so much and knows us so well, better than we know ourselves. He knows what we need to make our lives abundant, blessed, and full of love, which is what He desires for us. I know in my heart that Prophet brought Paul and me together in this lifetime to be married and to grow in love for God, ourselves, and each other. This is evident to me as I reflect on the experiences and steps we both were guided through by God to be where we are now. I know Paul and I knew each other in past lives and perhaps were married in other lifetimes, and that we both had a deep love for God and His Prophet, as we do now. This lifetime is a gift life for each of us, a blessing from the Divine, and a sweet reunion for Paul and me. Our marriage is built on the strong and sacred foundation of our love for God and His Prophet and by putting God first.

With deep love for and appreciation to God.

Written by Cathy Sandman

Paul and Cathy Summary

These teachings of God, lovingly given to us through His chosen Prophet, have enabled Cathy and me to share more openly with each other about everything, our dreams, concerns, and spiritual experiences. We support each other more, pray together more, and laugh together more.

God has miraculously healed each of us, and our marriage union. This does not mean now everything is smooth and easy. The challenges of life together still remain, and we each definitely have much more room to grow. The difference now is that we have been given the tools and experiences to prepare us and build our confidence. Each of us now has a closer and growing inner relationship with God's chosen Prophet of the times, and an attitude of gratitude to meet each daily challenge (opportunity) with God's help. A happy marriage requires purposeful effort. We still have to win our togetherness one day at a time, but it is *so worth it*!

Written by Paul and Cathy Sandman

7

Sacred Union
Shanna's Story

Have you ever wondered, "Why am I here? What is my purpose?" I know I did, and it wasn't until I began attending retreats at Guidance for a Better Life that the answers to these questions, and several more, began to transform my life in beautiful and abundant ways. Now I see it wasn't about finding "the answers" but learning what it means to live my life in a way that manifests the glories of God. I have come to know from personal experiences I have had at Guidance for a Better Life that we are here and we exist because of God's great Love for us. We are here in a physical embodiment to learn how to give and receive love, and a marriage is a beautiful place to grow in this Divine capacity. Recognizing and demonstrating the sacredness of a marriage founded in God fuels this purpose.

My story is more of a journey towards marriage than actual years of marriage. If someone had asked me ten years ago where I would see myself today it would not have involved being married, let alone writing about it. What a blessing it is that God knows our hearts better than we do, and so begins this section of my journey to growing in greater capacity to give and receive love.

I Knew She Was Special

I was twenty-two years of age when I met Tash. We were introduced through a mutual friend at a softball meeting. Her beauty immediately captured my attention as she walked up the last few stairs into the room where I was seated on a stool a few feet away. In truth, her beauty captured the attention of most people present in the room. I felt something special about her as we talked and got to know each other that first night. We set up our first date a few nights later. At that time I could not have imagined what an incredible gift God was bestowing upon me by bringing Tash into my life. I now know it was divinely inspired that we would cross paths again and continue our love story that began many years and lifetimes ago.

The examples of marriage I had as a child were not the best, but I trust they were perfect for my journey. My parents, whom I love dearly, were stuck in a destructive cycle of addiction to drugs and alcohol that eventually led to divorce. The custody battles lasted for years and are probably the most grueling part of a divorced family for all parties involved. To see the love two people once shared turn to hate and bitterness can be difficult for a child to comprehend and in my case bred a state of insecurity. Through their example marriage did not hold much value to me, and it would not be until meeting Del and Lynne Hall that this would begin to change.

Del and his wife Lynne are the first true examples I have had in putting God first in their life and in having a healthy, loving marriage. Their love for one another and for God radiates and shines. Being witness to this illuminated my heart to want to demonstrate this in my own life. It is through their example that I now recognize and appreciate the beauty, sweetness, and sacredness of a marriage founded in God.

Difficulty Expressing Myself

Some of my personal struggles have involved expression. As a child I found strength in keeping a fair amount of my opinions and emotions to myself. Between the addictions my parents struggled with and the custody battles, I found the less I said or shared the better things seemed to be in my life. What I had once considered to be a strength to help me through some seemingly tough times in my childhood had now become a weakness. My confidence in speaking up for myself and being clear and precise was lacking from years of suppression. There was much to be shared and expressed. I knew it was there, but I did not know how to nurture it.

I believe that when we help to bring out the best in our spouse it also helps to bring out the best in ourselves. To me this means recognizing and nurturing the beautiful qualities in one another. This helps nurture the sacredness in a marriage and in seeing one another as Soul. A few of the many beautiful qualities that Tash embodies are her generous and giving nature along with her ability to speak up and express herself. Through Tash I began to see the value and importance in speaking up and expressing things close to my heart. I yearned to do this but was having difficulty.

The Prophet's love for me as Soul saw through this wall of suppression I had placed on myself, and lovingly and gently helped me break this cycle. During a retreat he recommended that I find someone to help me with my communication and listening skills. This brought me to a "listening" doctor. This was an answer to a prayer in my heart. I had prayed to God and Prophet, asking for help and clarity in this area. I accepted my responsibility in creating a bottleneck situation through years of suppression, and I declared I was ready to break this mold and habit pattern. God will often bless us by guiding us to the people or doctors that can be used to help us.

I have been witness to how many of Prophet's suggestions to other students have blessed them. I knew to trust his advice and all the while knowing it came from a place of love. It was a genuine care in wanting what is best for one of his students, and it showed. The difficulty I had in expression had become a limiting factor in my spiritual growth and this affected my relationship with Tash and ultimately God. It is my experience that much of the love, help, and healings that I have received over the past decade from God through His Prophet have allowed me to experience greater states of freedom. The Prophet helps to unravel ties that tether Soul to the temporal things that hide its true and Divine nature.

God's Altar

In August of 2013 Tash and I moved to Virginia to be closer to the Guidance for a Better Life retreat center. I was really excited for our move because it had been a prayer in my heart to live closer to the retreat center for several years. Our move brought some changes to our way of life and our relationship. In the long run it was all for the better, but we did go through a bit of a rough patch. We even separated for a short period of time. This helped me see my priorities and know what I wanted in our relationship.

Some of our personal struggles had surfaced during this time. I know this was a blessing for both of us and that we had been conditioned over time to receive this gift. It was time to do away with the things in life that no longer served us as individuals and as a couple. Tash's struggle involved quitting drinking and for me it was learning to speak up and express myself. Through this less than pleasant time in our relationship, a bigger unanswered question had finally surfaced from the depths of my heart. "Is God really okay with my relationship with Tash?" Which when I took it even deeper turned into this question, "Am I truly worthy of God and His Love because of my love for her?" The childhood years I had spent going to Catholic and Christian churches with my family had bred a deep insecurity that I was not worthy and would be condemned to hell "for all eternity" for loving someone of the same sex. This never really rang true to me, but when supposed "people of God" preach this message it can have an impact and inadvertently put a wall between an individual and God.

It was not until Prophet shattered this facade by showing me that God does truly love me and loves all of His children, and that this insecurity could be healed. Prophet has respected and treated Tash and me as Soul, and in doing this it helped us see our own divinity. He didn't look down on us like we have lived in sin. Through God's Love that flows through him, Prophet has always helped to remove any wedges between

God and me, not place them. I feel as though he saw the love between us, as Soul, and nurtured that through many years. This has been a process, with each step just as important as the next. Prophet has helped heal deep insecurities, and demonstrated that what he teaches truly is the path of Divine love.

The Altar of God Experience

There came a point where I wanted the truth about my relationship with Tash, and I was willing to give it up if that is what was truly right with God. One evening after singing HU, a beautiful love song to God, I was in contemplation and was joined by the inner presence of the Prophet. As I looked into Prophet's eyes, God's Grace showered over us, raising me up spiritually. I saw myself before the Altar of God with Prophet by my side. I knelt in humility and declared, "Thy will be done." When I placed our relationship on the Altar of God, which speaks to me of truly surrendering, the insecurity no longer had me, God did!

God was never asking me to give up my relationship with Tash but rather my attachment to it. My attachment was based on fear and not in the nobility of Divine love that I'd been shown by example countless times through His Prophet, Del. A realization flourished in my heart that God does not use the labels that man does. We are all so self-limiting when we put on labels made by society or the so-called religious experts.

Married by God's Prophet

I surprised Tash and myself when speaking up and asking Del if he would be willing to officiate our wedding ceremony. We were at a retreat in February 2014 and the topic of marriage had come up. I felt drawn to put it out there. It was not even legal at the time in our state. Del shared that he would be happy to marry Tash and me when it became legal. It is difficult to put into words just how deeply this touched me. I believe some of the courage I felt in asking came from the healings I experienced in placing my relationship on God's Altar and the help I received in speaking up and expressing myself. Del shared that more and more states are making it legal and it is just a matter of time. He said, "I think the law will be changing here soon." This proved to be true when eight months later the state of Virginia allowed same sex marriages. We formally asked Del at a retreat in November 2014 if he would do us the honor and privilege in officiating our marriage ceremony. With love in his eyes he accepted and we set our wedding day for the following summer. It is no coincidence to me that he spoke the law would be changing soon and it did.

July 18, 2015 is one of the most beautiful and incredible days of my life because it is the day I was blessed to marry Tash. On this sacred and special day I stood with my soon to be wife, in the company of many cherished loved ones, as God's Light and Love surrounded us. She looked stunning and radiant. The Divine presence and love that emanated and flowed through Prophet manifested a piece of Heaven on Earth.

This brought reverence into our wedding day and the truth of God's Love for Soul blossomed in my heart at a deeper level and became a greater reality in my life. As I said before, there is something very special about being recognized and loved as Soul. Prophet agreeing to officiate our wedding ceremony spoke to me of what it means to be loved for who we truly are, fellow children of God, and not what society would label us as.

There is a part in the wedding ceremony where Prophet says, "Kneel and open your hearts to love. Kneeling expresses humility before God and each other." The Love of God that flowed to us from the eyes of the Prophet upon kneeling uplifted me spiritually. The sacredness of our holy matrimony had been established and recognized in God's eyes. I knew this in my heart for my very being resounded in this truth and I became consumed by love, Divine love. Love so intense that it could annihilate me yet so profound and gentle that it held me together.

From our wedding ceremony I took home a tool to help resolve conflicts that arise in disagreements between my spouse and me. I go back to the experience of us kneeling and remember what it was like to humble myself before God, Prophet, and my wife. This seems to diffuse the emotional entanglements I may have in a disagreement. It makes me feel vulnerable and completely safe at the same time. There is an indescribable beauty in this act that can only be understood in its demonstration. It brings me back to love and gratitude, allowing me to once again see my wife as Soul, and then reverence flows. It helps bring back the sacredness of our marriage and love for one another and helps us to move on. Disagreements and arguments are going to happen, but this tool has been helpful for us to work out a more constructive resolution.

Our experience in being able to finally get married transformed our relationship to experience a deeper level of commitment. Tash and I were together for twelve years before marriage and I did not expect much to change, but there was a difference. Our marriage made things sweeter and it added a layer of security that I did not know was missing. I can see how this also applies to my relationship with God and God's Prophet. Being married and "all in" makes for true security. For me, putting God first and being secure in my spiritual marriage blesses my physical marriage.

As I mentioned earlier, the labels we use for ourselves and for others are very limiting and create separateness among individuals. Labels help the mind of man put things in a box, but they hide the boundlessness of Soul. Society often uses labels to separate people into categories. My story is not about being gay or straight or any label but shared to express that God loves all of us dearly, and when we love another Soul in a way that is uplifting it helps fuel the fire for the Love of God in our hearts. In my experience, if a marriage is founded in love for God and one another then it is blessed!

As Prophet has graciously and unceasingly taught and shown me at every single retreat, so I say unto you once again, "You exist because God loves you. You are Soul, a child of God, a spark of the Divine. As Soul you are eternal and boundless. Be grateful for everything you have." You can carry this with you in your marriage and in your life and I know it will bless you and others. The Prophet has, over many years, helped to remove the labels I have placed on myself and now I not only know I am Soul, but I also try to live my life in a way that demonstrates this truth.

Heaven is real and I see it at times in the eyes of my wife as God's Love flows through her. I believe our marriage founded in God, through Prophet, has the potential to bring a little bit of Heaven to Earth when we love and respect one another. A reverence and sacredness for my wife and our marriage helps manifest some of the glories of God on Earth.

The Prophet of our times, Del Hall III, has made all of this possible because he saw my wife and I as Soul. This may sound like such a simple statement, but the magnitude of God's Prophet seeing and loving us, as Soul, is astounding in cultivating a heart that sings to be an instrument of God. When someone truly sees and loves you, as Soul, it is life changing. It has inspired me to be the best "me" I can be.

My hope in sharing part of my story with you, dear reader, is that it will help manifest a piece of Heaven in your own marriage by the reverence that flows from nurturing the sacredness of your holy union founded in God. One of the best ways to do this is in building a conscious relationship with the Prophet of our times. You do not need to "get married" on the first date. My ever-growing spiritual marriage with God and Prophet has been a process over many years. It truly is one of God's greatest blessings in my life and in my marriage.

Written by Shanna Canine

8

Sacred Union
Tash's Story

Driving to one of my first weeklong retreats at Guidance for a Better Life in 2006 I saw a church sign that said: "Change is inevitable, growth is optional." I believe that is true. I have learned the value of putting God first and accepting that change is an inevitable part of living in the physical world. Our body ages; every material item we buy is decaying before we even get it out of the package. Health, finances, and homes all can change. The good news is we are eternal and that doesn't change. We *are* Soul, a Divine spark of God, and we *have* a body.

Soul is happy and at peace. Learning to operate as Soul and see my spouse this way is one of the keys to our joyful marriage. Soul can live comfortably with change while enjoying the stability of a life rooted in God. With this way of life comes growth. This way of life was taught to me by Del Hall, Prophet of our times. I hope to pass it on to you.

Love in a Box

There are Hallmark movies on the subject of love. Go to any card shop and you will have plenty of love poems to choose from, yet I wonder if we use that word so often that we are desensitized to its true magnitude. Love and certainly marriage can fall into complacency if a conscious effort is not made to affirm its sacred value daily and grow in our understanding of it.

I wonder if at times we put love in a box on the shelf and assume we know what it is all about. Perhaps we could blow off that *dusty box*, open it up, and take another look. We might see infinite depths worth falling into, never to be reached entirely. Love cannot be put into any box if it is to grow or truly be experienced. Growth is impossible without change. The core of our love does not have to change, but perhaps we can experience a greater quality of love if we choose to grow together and make God a priority in our life.

I used to think I knew what love was. I did on some level, but there was so much more. When I realized one of the reasons I was alive was to learn how to give and receive Divine love, I prayed in sincerity to Prophet, and it changed my life for the better. "Teach me how to love," I asked. A whole new world opened up for me after this. A wave of gratitude cascaded over the seemingly mundane aspects of my life. I aspired to love in a way that would make God smile. Now love is something I demonstrate. It is not a feeling dependent on my mood. It is not a fleeting and fickle sensation. Now I allow others to do things for me as I do for them. I am able to accept compliments better than I used to be able to.

I have learned that feeling love for someone is one thing. Being able to demonstrate it in a way that allows them to experience your love is another. It requires more than simply saying "I love you." This is not to suggest that saying it is not necessary or reassuring, but if that is all we do the message will be less impactful. A student at Guidance for a Better Life once used the words "Actions express our priorities," and I think this is true for love as well as everything else. For example, if your spouse is speaking to you, stop what you are doing and listen. This is a demonstration of love. Every once in awhile remember to express gratitude rather than complaints. It is important to balance your corrections with gratitude. In many ways gratitude expressed is the doorway to love.

"Happily ever after" is a fairy tale because it suggests that once you find love, you are all set. Just fall in love, get married, and enjoy a lifetime of happiness together. Love alone is not enough. It takes devotion and responsibility to make a marriage last. I believe it also takes a foundation in God.

My Journey to Marriage

Marriage is no longer strictly a union between a man and a woman. Marriage now includes people of the same sex. Perhaps a new definition of marriage could be, "a sacred union between two Souls blessed by God." It is a special opportunity and I am grateful that it became available for us.

My wife Shanna and I found each other in January 2003 out of two common interests; growing spiritually and living a life rooted in God. We would spend hours talking about God, life after death, reincarnation, and other topics of interest. We seemed to be helping each other "wake up" from a spiritual slumber. Our prior relationships were devoid of such talks. I found Shanna to be intellectually stimulating, but it was deeper than that. Something inside me stirred in her presence and I liked it. A year after we began dating we were introduced to Guidance for a Better Life in 2004 by my aunt and uncle. There we met the greatest teacher of God's ways, Del Hall III.

Our story is more about a journey to marriage rather than many years of marriage. We lived together for twelve years prior to being able to legally get married. Although we waited many years for that special day, marriage is not just a day of celebration but a lifetime of demonstration. There is hope for your marriage if it is troubled. Having faith, believing in, and accepting Prophet made our lives abundant in every way. This is what made marriage and true love possible for us.

For many years of my life, my father was addicted to alcohol, and my mother became depressed. They were passionate and equally talented, had interests in art, literature, medicinal herbs, and organic gardening, which they passed on to us. I am not a victim at all and have compassion for their struggles. Raising children and trying to *survive* was not easy. Couples argue. People disagree. That is going to happen sometimes. Having a skillset to navigate through those times and reach productive resolution to conflicts is worth learning. My mom and dad did not have those tools.

Unfortunately, their marriage became an example of what happens when past hurts are not forgiven. My father does not drink anymore and has apologized for the past. Still, there is a canyon between my parents' hearts. She feels misunderstood and lonely and so does he.

Their biggest challenge is communication skills. Their conversations end in fights a lot so they do not talk much anymore. I can remember several times from age five to seven, my mother would pack up our stuff and say we were leaving. Sometimes she would threaten to leave and never come back. This frightened me and left me feeling insecure. I decided to become self-reliant and independent so as not to *need* anyone. I felt I had to do everything for myself because I could not count on anyone.

In spite of their issues they did not divorce and still live together in the same house but separately. Growing up I always had good food, a roof over my head, and I knew I was loved. I love my parents. They did the best they could.

As soon as I was able to leave home and get a place of my own I did. Living with people who do not get along is not pleasant. It produces a lot of anxiety because you never know when a fight is going to break out. Perhaps my parents loved each other at one time, I am not sure. They did not demonstrate it in front of me. I did not have an example of a healthy marriage growing up.

The first example I witnessed of a loving marriage where two people put God first was Del and Lynne Hall. I do not recall a specific discourse on marriage per se, but their love of God and each other shone through as they served one another joyfully, each in their own ways. It was clear that following the teachings produced a happy marriage. Finally, I knew this kind of love existed and was possible. Could our relationship be like that? I wondered. A seed was planted.

Just before meeting Shanna, I turned twenty-nine years old. My first attempt at love had ended poorly after eight years. Like my parents, I lacked the communication skills to successfully navigate through conflicts. As long as there were no disagreements I was fine, but when there were I would get defensive and try to win the argument. I would speak louder and louder, eventually yelling, and slamming doors. I felt inept, to say the least. Even if I had a good point, I would end up having to apologize for whatever I said or did during the disagreement, so my points were often forgotten, leaving me back to square one.

This behavior was unappealing to me yet I was not able to control myself at times. I wanted to do better. I was constantly searching for ways to improve myself. I had tried everything from various religious teachings, meditation, anger management, traditional counseling, life coaching, and self-improvement seminars. They did help to get me to a certain point. I was outwardly successful by some standards but inwardly flailing. I felt I had to prove myself time and time again. I was anxious and always trying to accomplish the next goal. I never felt good enough. I was not at peace.

I Almost Lost Her

Through Shanna I began to realize that all those things I was trying so hard to *be* I already *was.* In her eyes, there was no distance between me and all those goals. I was good enough just as I was. She saw the real me, Soul. It would be many more years before I saw it for myself; even more before I would consistently operate from this place. Shanna was stable in every sense of that word. God's Love flowed effortlessly from her. Gentle, strong, and wise, she was outwardly beautiful, yet what I saw was radiating out from within. Her love inspired me and uplifted me. I would not be where I am today without her example. She rarely judged me or told me how to act. This was refreshing.

Shanna and I dated for six months and then went on a vacation to Saint Croix together. The vacation went great, but she seemed too good to be true. I allowed what other people thought to over ride my gut instincts. I had a life coach at the time and she advised me that Shanna was too young for me (she was twenty-two and I was just turning thirty). I did what the life coach thought I should, which was end the relationship before I got too far into it. Lesson learned. All consultants are just that. I now take their advice into consideration but follow my inner knowingness.

The day I broke up with Shanna I knew I had made a mistake. My stomach was in knots and I could not get over how I felt. I prayed to God for guidance and decided to sleep on it. For not knowing someone very long, I was surprised by how difficult our break up was. The next day I had a strong sense I needed to try to make up with her. I called several times and she never answered. I knew she was avoiding my calls. I finally left a message for her to call me back.

Late that evening she called me. I prayed for a sign so that I would know if she was "the one." During our phone discussion Shanna shared a dream with me that was the answer to my prayers. After she shared the dream, I knew that she was someone I had known in a prior life. Years later, during inner experiences guided by Del, I found out we had indeed shared a love connection before.

Shanna's Dream

Before falling asleep that night she prayed for a spiritual guide to comfort and help heal the hurt in her heart from the breakup. A peace-filled being of light and love appeared to her in the dream state. I was in the dream with her and we were in a place filled with light. This peaceful Soul seemed to be a spiritual Master. He showed her past lives we had been in together and she saw the possibility of a future life together as a married couple. He instructed us to turn and face one another. "See one another as I see you," he said. As we looked into each other's eyes our physical bodies faded away, transforming into bright light. All became light and love surrounding us, yet we recognized one another.

When she shared this dream, I knew that she was "the one." I asked her to forgive me. She did and we started over with a new understanding of ourselves. We were not male or female really. We were Souls made of light and love. This has always been part of the foundation of our relationship.

Growing and Maturing

As a child we did not attend church as a family. Nature was our "church" which I enjoyed. However some part of me craved structure and wanted God's teachings. For awhile in middle school, I went with a good friend and studied the Bible a bit. I was drawn to be close with God, yet what I had experienced of religion seemed incomplete, like important truths were missing. Obviously this was not a reflection of Jesus. Where was the part about living more than one life? I knew that we did. How could a loving God send his children to "hell" for eternity? Even at a young age I had questions. I loved God and loved Jesus, yet I did not feel like I belonged in any orthodox religion.

I tried to *just be normal* and dated men here and there, but that was only to please people and avoid judgment. I was not happy doing that, and it seemed like I was living a lie. I eventually accepted that I was "gay." Even now it is hard to say that. The label is so limiting and conjures up opinions and judgments and puts me into a box. I identify as Soul, not as a label. The transient aspects of my outer life do not define me, nor do they diminish me. The experiences are a part of my personal journey back home to the Heart of God. I am grateful for the lessons I have had, and along the way I was blessed to find true love.

My biggest challenge had become an attachment to alcohol, having a couple drinks almost daily from the time I was twenty-one until thirty-eight. I was able to quit off and on for a month or two but never longer. I became mentally obsessed with it and looked forward to "happy hour" every day. Although I rarely got drunk I began to wonder if I was an alcoholic; another label I do not place on myself but a gentle reminder that I never want to go back to that old life.

I have changed. The issues that used to plague my relationships: drinking, insecurity, and always needing to have the last word in an argument are nearly gone. I tried everything I knew of to change myself for the better, but nothing had the transformational effect that being in the presence of the Prophet produced. Tools without God's Prophet will only get you so far. Some of these negative molds were so deeply engrained that without the Prophet's healing help I would not be rid of them. I did my part to accept and nurture the changes, but I could not have done it without God's Grace.

A big turning point for me came years into being a student at the Guidance for a Better Life. I had gathered enough courage Guidance for a Better Life and trust during one of the retreats to put my life on the "Altar of God." This meant truly surrendering everything that I held dear and even what I did not. I wanted God's will for my life more than my own will. I wanted more than knowledge. I wanted to know and understand truth. I prayed anything that was not right for me be made clear so that I could take action.

It became clear that we needed to move to Virginia now and not wait. We lived in Maryland at this time and I had a business that was fourteen years matured. Leaving and starting over seemed daunting. I had a condo that I had been trying to sell for two years. The homeowners association was not getting enough dues because of the housing crash in 2008. It meant the people who were paying their dues had to pay much more to cover the foreclosed properties. This made my condo difficult to sell at current market value because it added another four hundred dollars per month to the cost of ownership. Over the years I had invested in improvements so I was attached to getting at least some of that money back.

Instead of getting better, it was getting worse. The dues kept increasing. Finally I went to my realtor and conceded that I would go ahead with a short sale and take a loss. I knew I needed to let go of this place and move forward. I wanted to be closer to Prophet both physically and inwardly. I had to let go of "the old life" and accept "the new life" God had for us.

It also became clear that I needed to quit drinking once and for all. During some solo time at a retreat I wrote a letter asking Prophet to help me be rid of my drinking problem. What once brought comfort and relief was now a wedge between God, Shanna, and me. I had the means to rely on Prophet, yet I habitually went to the drink instead. This was also getting between Shanna and me as it was making me more withdrawn and self-indulgent. She needed me to be present and I was not. I did not send the letter, but I knew I had been heard. I surrendered the outcome and forgot about the petition for help. I never gave up trying to quit alcohol.

We moved to Virginia and I worked hard to get my practice up and running like it was in Maryland. My work is rewarding but physically demanding. I ran a special to gain new customers and doubled my workload to compensate for the decrease in pay. I was working too much, had poor boundaries, and allowed myself to become stressed out and get out of balance. I could relate to the Bible quote, "Be sober, be vigilant; because your adversary the devil, as a roaring lion, walketh about, seeking whom he may devour:" 1 Peter 5:8 KJV In hindsight I was trying to do everything myself. I had asked Prophet for help inwardly but was not truly trusting. In a moment of weakness I drank again, breaking my promise to God, Shanna, and myself. Shanna and I went through a brief period of separation during this time as we were both uncertain of our future together and needed clarity.

While attending another weeklong retreat I had a dream which showed me more truth about my drinking problem. The message I got from this dream was that my attachment to this habit was an open door which would allow *the thief* to steal everything dear to me. I had a vision of where my life would be if I chose to continue breaking my promises, if only for "one time."

I did not volunteer to share the dream because everyone had heard this issue before. I was sick of hearing about it and I was sure the class was too. I thought that the problem was behind me. My uncle, also a student of Del, shared his dream in class which had me in it. My uncle's dream put my dream in play. Del turned his attention to me. At this point I had been sober for six months, sincerely doing my best. I truly wanted to be free of this. Prophet knew my heart.

Not knowing what else to do, I instinctively knelt on the floor in front of my chair, exhausted with this issue. Inwardly I begged forgiveness with what seemed like lifetimes of guilt in my heart. I felt every part of myself opening to God. There was so much I had been carrying. I had no idea. I had never really "let go" until this moment. On my knees before the whole class I finally surrendered. With the full power of God's mercy Del, the Prophet, intervened on my behalf and broke the shackles of this addiction; healing me, washing away years of broken promises, guilt, regret, shame, and denial. I felt truly "reborn" after this.

As I sat up from the floor I realized what I was thirsting for had been in front of me for years. I had looked at Del many times but with that wedge removed, it was as if I finally "saw" him. God's Presence poured through him, It's Divine channel. He is the water of life. It was as if a dam had burst around me and my heart flooded with love for the Divine authority that flowed from him. This love flowed into my heart and back out to Prophet.

When I truly surrendered in genuine humility I seemed to gain everything. An elevation in my understanding of who Del is and what he teaches came. He had always been trying to free me from excessive attachments, labels, insecurity, vanity, anger, fear, doubt, unworthiness, and lies. Love is not a big enough word to describe what I saw in his eyes, yet it was all this and more. This had a positive effect on every painful symptom that resulted from the wedge between God, His Prophet, and me. My relationship with Shanna was so much better. I was inspired to give back to God and devote my life to Him whole-heartedly. I began to demonstrate love, not just talk about it. I began to give of myself in greater ways.

Following this healing, more truth was revealed to me. I had fears I hadn't faced. I had questions I was not aware of. These were another wedge between God and me. "What if once I get to a certain point on the path God asks me to give up my relationship with Shanna? What if God's will is for me to be straight and He is just waiting for me to be strong enough to do the right thing?" I never realized how much these fears were holding me back. I played very small because I was afraid of getting to that "point," wherever it was. I did not want to lose Shanna, but I needed to know the truth whatever it was.

God, Prophet, Shanna, and Me

As I said in the beginning of my story we do not "have" a Soul we "are" Soul. The qualities of Soul are Divine. These are peace, freedom, love, joy, wisdom, compassion, strength, loyalty, and more. These God-like qualities are in all of us and it is what we truly are. However, these attributes are not activated until Prophet does so. Only Prophet can open the window of Heaven for us. We must be conditioned to accept such a gift. Much like my early struggles, it is not always comfortable.

When I read about the process of extracting gold from a compound mass I was reminded of the journey of Soul. It is not subjected to the process of fusion only once. The alloy must be melted in the crucible several times before the gold is released in all its purity. Life is good. We live many lifetimes. It may not always be fun or easy, but it is how we learn. We need experiences.

Some of my wife's challenges involved speaking up and expressing herself. There were times when I felt lonely with her because of this. I wanted to hear her thoughts, opinions, and dreams, but at our lowest point she had withdrawn into a cocoon of silence, and I was like a bird pecking away relentlessly at the shell, trying to get her to come out. When Shanna and I are out of balance, she tends to get passive and procrastinate, and I am impatient and make rash decisions. This is why living a life rooted in God is so important. God is the only real stability there is. When we put God first our life is in balance and harmony.

She has gotten help with these issues and to my surprise she boldly spoke up on our behalf during a retreat and changed the course of our lives. It was a winter weekend retreat and the subject of marriage came up. Shanna spontaneously asked Del if it ever became legal would he officiate our wedding. With her question, the tiniest seed of a dream sprouted within me. For the first time in my life I allowed myself to imagine what that might be like for us. Del thought carefully and spoke the words out loud: Times were changing and he thought that it would be possible soon. Several months later the law in our state changed, and several months after that the Supreme Court ruled in favor of our freedom to marry and have it recognized nationally rather than state by state.

Del, God's chosen Prophet, made our marriage possible and gave us his blessing on July 18, 2015. There is no one else I would have wanted to officiate for us. I will always remember his kindness in giving us such a gift. Today my love for Shanna is a reflection of my love for God. They build on each other. I know without a doubt that God is okay with our marriage. This foundation helps if people disagree. It does not matter to me any more man's opinion of me or my marriage. I am at peace. Those old fears have been put to rest. If a marriage is based on love, mutual respect, and God, it is blessed.

We now have what I consider a love triangle where God is at the top and Shanna and I are at each corner. As we grow closer to God we grow closer with each other. Without Prophet's help old patterns of behavior we came into this lifetime with and picked up along the way would not be broken, and no hope for lasting growth would be possible. Prophet does not interfere in our lives unless invited. He is a guide and shows us the way. He never pushes himself on anyone regardless of how much we may need him to. This is because he respects us and our God-given free will.

Spiritual travel with Prophet to God's Temples on the inner planes revealed that Shanna and I have been married before in a past lifetime many thousands of years ago. Our love is enduring. We were in male and female bodies at that time, deeply in love and very happy. We have also had a lifetime as young brothers although she died many years before me in that life. Our past connection is based in love, but still there are things we work through in order to keep our love alive. Prophet's guidance and presence over time untied karmic patterns and allowed Shanna and me to be free to develop new healthy ways of relating to each other. Many times we may want to act in love, but deep-rooted weeds from the past can choke out even the best intentions.

One of the aspects of God's teachings is that

being passive is not productive. A marriage can have a "love triangle" and still not last if both people are not equally committed to actively doing their part to nurture the blessings. In the beginning the change and growth were rapid for me, and it was difficult at times but absolutely worth it. I am at a peaceful and relaxed pace now, but there are refined changes taking place. Being receptive to them is helpful.

During one part of our marriage ceremony, Del instructed us to kneel and express humility to one another and to God as he gave us a blessing. We knelt before him, encompassed in the radiant light and love that surrounded us in his presence. I experienced solace before him. He said that each of us was equal in the eyes of God. When we are having a disagreement I imagine myself on my knees before the Prophet and God; before my beloved. This expression of humility allows me to have clarity. It puts the ego in its place and breaks the destructive habit I had of trying to *win arguments*. Remembering that ego makes its appearance when I am feeling insecure is helpful. I remind myself that I am loved just as I am and there is nothing to prove. Imagining or actually physically getting on your knees is helpful if you have this habit.

For example, we do not quarrel often

anymore, but once while we were in an argument I felt old habits creeping in. I made a conscious decision to go into another room. I shut the door. I was upset in the moment and wanted clarity. I simply knelt down. Instantly I knew that our fight was ridiculous. It was put into perspective. I had done everything I could do. All that was left was to let go. I trusted and peace came into my heart again. Afterward, we were able to speak more gently and listen to one another again. The result was amazing, but it does take awareness and self-discipline to remember to do it. This comes with practice.

All of my life has been a process of learning, accepting change, and growing, and it is all *spiritual.* I see marriage in the same way. Some think marriage is just a "piece of paper," but it is different than living together. It is a deeper commitment, and I find peace and security in my physical marriage and in my marriage with the Divine.

We are works in progress and we are at peace with that. We have come a long way from where we used to be. Through integrating the teachings into our lives and accepting Del's help, I can say that we operate more from our God-like nature, as Soul, and not the human nature. There is a difference between human nature and

Divine nature. We do our best each day. We continue to do everything we did to get to this point to nurture our blessings. We are content in our life together, but we are not complacent. As nice as it is to be comfortable, we know that we must be alert for complacency.

Shanna and I have grown so much that we now have to take a "new picture of ourselves" and remember not to anticipate the old behaviors. We have to be in the moment of now. We have grown as individuals but become closer than ever because we put God first.

It has been four years since we moved in August 2012. Jesus' disciples left everything to follow him. I felt the same urge calling to me when I knew that it was time to leave Maryland and move to Virginia to be closer to today's Prophet. I could never have known how incredibly blessed our life would be. I did not expect to be married. We are so happy. We bought a home together with a little land, have true friends who share our spiritual interests, and have the tools to keep growing closer. My practice is doing well now and I am past the initial start-up challenges. We are living in God's promises of true peace, happiness, and abundance. Our life is in balance. Change does not have to be feared. We do not dwell on where we used to be, but the remembrance of it fuels the appreciation to nurture this new life. There is more for us; always one more step and always more truth and love to be accepted. There is more for you if you want it.

Summary of Tools and Helpful Contemplations

Of anything I have shared, the most valuable would be accepting a conscious relationship with the Prophet of our times. This will grow over time and you do not have to "get married" on the first date. Like any relationship it takes time, effort, and trust to build. Love and abundance follow. Positive changes will come from taking responsibility for your part and giving what you cannot do to him. An understanding of God's language and how much you are loved will be expressed to you in dreams, everyday life, spiritual travel, and more. You do not have to be "all in" right away, but with Prophet's help you too can grow to trust God enough to put your hopes, fears, and dreams on His Altar. If something is good and right for you, it will be blessed and you will know it. You will find God's Grace helping you and leading you through your conflicts to greater wisdom and a greater capacity to love.

Singing HU is a daily practice that uplifts and opens us up to higher ways of doing things. We do this daily.

Be honest with yourself. Even if you are not ready to make a change, being honest with yourself can be helpful. Do you have excessive attachments to things, outcomes, people, opinions, old attitudes, etc. that you allow to steal your peace and control you?

Setting and keeping boundaries is important. Is your life out of balance, or some area of your life? If so are you willing to do what it takes to get in balance?

Over the years I have actively sought to be a more effective communicator and better listener. It has taken time. I find that dealing with conflicts as they come up is more helpful than ignoring them or pretending they are not there. I do this by asking permission to discuss something that is bothering me. I used to just blurt things out whenever it suited me and that did not go well. Now I make sure that Shanna is receptive to the conversation beforehand and it ends in productive resolution.

Sometimes I simply remember my blessings. I find it helpful. Remember why you wanted to get married in the first place. What qualities do you love about your spouse? Do you still want to be married? If so, are there things you would like to change? Perhaps you can invite Prophet to help you with your marriage (and your life) as he has helped us. Ask Prophet to help you have clarity and strength to move forward. Are you willing to take responsibility for your part and do whatever you are being led to do?

Do not stop asking for truth and clarity. We are both quick to forgive, to apologize, take responsibility, and move on. This is so helpful and I appreciate this quality in our marriage.

"Daily Bread" and drawing nigh to God; we don't dwell on this, but if we are not spiritually nourished daily and actively feeding ourselves it is easy to fall prey to the negative forces down here. We can be polarized towards God or towards "the other guy." Do not allow anything to become a wedge between you, your spouse, and God. Stay alert and vigilant. Do not passively allow that to happen.

Every thought, word, and action has an impact. Destructive thoughts, language, and actions can undermine your daily spiritual exercises and leave you as malnourished as if you never did them in the first place. If you make a promise do not even imagine breaking it. What we think becomes our attitude and our attitudes become our behavior.

Before bed you could ask for a dream in which you see yourselves as Soul. You can also do an exercise while awake where you look into each other's eyes for at least twenty minutes. Face one another and ask Prophet to help you see your spouse as they truly are. Ask to see through his eyes.

Written by Tash Canine

Sacred Union Summary

It has been said, "The best things come to those who wait." We would like to rephrase that: "The best things come to those who wait on the Lord." Putting God first has blessed every area of our lives including our marriage. We were careful not to get caught up in a "poor me" attitude for not having the "right" to get married. We moved on and lived our lives as Prophet taught us.

Prophet taught us to get our minds off ourselves and think of others. He showed us that love is not separate from serving and giving to one another. Our true nature is to be used by God to be a blessing to others. We surrender our hopes, fears, and dreams to God and when the timing is right for us, if it is in our best spiritual interest, our gifts are given. We worked on our issues but did not obsess over them. Most of our healing came when we let go and surrendered to God's will.

We know that we truly are Soul, regardless of any labels used to identify us or how many times our bodies die. We know that our love is eternal. We will see each other again. Living life this way and knowing this truth makes accepting

Prophet's guidance and putting God first the only secure investment that creates a truly abundant life.

We are grateful for Del and Lynne Hall and appreciate their example of a healthy marriage. It is through their example that we recognize the beauty, sweetness, and sacredness of a marriage founded in God. Having reverence for God nurtures having reverence for your spouse.

For us it is not about living up to society's standard of what a perfect marriage looks like. It is not about "doing it right." It is about "being right" with God through His Prophet. We are not perfect and sometimes we have off days. We simply strive to have hearts that are open and ready to accept an apology when it is given and the humility to give an apology when needed.

We will continue to nurture our love connection with God, Prophet, and each other. We truly appreciate our marriage and the opportunities that it brings for us in this life together. We hope to inspire you to take on the attitude that marriage truly is a sacred gift from God if it is rooted in Divine love and this love is demonstrated daily.

Written by Tash and Shanna Canine

Guidance for a Better Life
Our Story

My Father's Journey

God always has a living Prophet on earth to teach His Ways and accomplish His Will. My father, Del Hall III, is currently God's true Prophet fully raised up and ordained by God Himself. He was not always a Prophet, nor did he even know what a Prophet was, but God had a plan

Prophet Del Hall III

for him like He has for all of His children. Over many years through many life experiences, God had begun to prepare my father for his future assignment, mostly unbeknownst to him.

Everything he experienced in his life from the joys to the sadness helped prepare him for his future role as Prophet.

My dad grew up in California and was a decent student but a better athlete. He received an appointment to the United States Naval Academy in Annapolis, Maryland where he later met my mother. They were married two days after he graduated and received his commission as an officer. After a short tour on a Navy ship deployed to Vietnam, he went to flight training school and became a navy fighter pilot. While attending flight school in Pensacola, Florida he also earned a Master of Science Degree and had the first of his three children, a son. After flight school he was stationed in a fighter squadron on the east coast, where he and my mom began investing in real estate, adding to their family with the birth of two daughters. Following this tour of duty he was assigned as a jet flight instructor in Texas, after which, his time in the Navy was finished. He was a natural pilot and loved his time in the sky, but it was time to move on.

So far in life he had no real concern for, or even thought much about God, religion, or spiritual matters in general. He lived life fully. He raised his family. He traveled. He invested and became an entrepreneur starting and growing highly successful businesses in diverse fields ranging from real estate to aerospace consulting. Years before however, a seed had been planted when God's eternal teachings were introduced to him in his late teens, and while it did not show outwardly, the truth in these teachings spoke to his heart. My dad might not have been giving much thought to God up to this point in his life, but God was definitely thinking about him and the future He had planned for him. Like an acorn destined to become a mighty oak, the seed that lay dormant in his heart would someday be stirred to life. Through all his life experiences, both "good" and "bad," God would be preparing him for his future role as His Prophet.

When God decided it was time, He called my dad to Him. He did this by shutting down the world of financial security my dad had built. Over a period of two years all of his businesses were wound down and dissolved. What seemed like security turned out to be an illusion. Financial success had not provided true security. He now had failed businesses and a failing marriage and was trying to fix things without God's help, principles, or guidance. As painful as this time in his life was, it was yet another step towards the glorious life of service awaiting my father. God was removing him from the world my dad had created and furthering him along his path to his future role as Prophet.

After his marriage ended and his businesses wound down, he started fresh by going out west to give flying lessons near Lake Mead, Nevada. While living in Nevada my dad was reintroduced to the eternal teachings of God he first learned of as a teenager twenty-three years earlier, and though they resonated with him at the time, his priorities were different back then. Now, his serious training could begin. He started having very clear experiences with the Holy Spirit and noticed there was a familiarity with these teachings and experiences. He embraced the long hours of instruction, which often lasted until sunrise, and was receptive to the personal spiritual experiences he was given. This began an intense period of study and desire for spiritual truth that continues to this day. Some of his most profound and meaningful experiences during this time were with past Prophets of old. They came to him spiritually in contemplations and dreams. He learned of their roles in history and how they were raised up and ordained by God directly. He began to realize they were training him but was not clear why. A few times his experiences led him to believe he was in training to be a future Prophet. However, that revelation made no sense to him because he felt he was an imperfect person who made mistakes and had failures. He thought of the past and current Prophets of God as perfected Souls, not imperfect like he felt he was. Why would God choose him for such a role? He did not feel qualified.

Besides being introduced to God's teachings while he was out west, my father was blessed to meet his current wife Lynne. Returning to the East Coast, my father and Lynne moved into a small cabin on land he had acquired before his businesses shut down. This was a major change in his life, but it felt deeply right within him. He began to remember a desire to live like this as a child; from early childhood my dad found clarity and peace in nature. He had forgotten about this until now, but God had not and made this dream a reality. In addition to being their home, these beautiful, three-hundred-plus acres of land in the Blue Ridge Mountains would eventually become the location for the Guidance for a Better Life retreat center. The perfection of my father's experiences from earlier in his life in real estate, providing the land for his next step in life, speak to the perfection of God's plan. One of many many examples I could list.

For many years my dad took wilderness skills courses around the country. He specialized in the study of wild edible and medicinal plants, tracking, and awareness skills, and authored articles for publication. Inspired to help folks feel more comfortable in the outdoors, my dad and Lynne began the Nature Awareness School in 1990. Classes were focused on teaching awareness and the primitive living skills needed to enjoy the woods and survive in them if necessary. An amazing thing happened within those first few years though; students began to experience aspects of God in very personal and dramatic ways. Somewhat like my dad's experience out west, they found that stepping away from their daily routine and the hustle of life, if even for a few days, created space for Spirit to do Its work. Whether they were enjoying the beauty of the Virginia wilderness and tranquility of the school grounds or relaxing by the pond, he found students' hearts opened, and they became more receptive to the Divine Hand that is always reaching out to Its children.

More and more the discourse during wilderness classes shifted to the meanings of dreams, personal growth, finding balance in life, and experiences the students were having with the Voice of God in Its many forms. An increase of spiritual retreats was offered to fulfill the demand and over time became the predominant class offerings; the wilderness survival skills classes eventually fading away completely. The name "Nature Awareness School" seemed to be less fitting for what was actually being taught now and in February 2019 my father changed the name of the retreat center to Guidance for a Better Life.

Throughout this time my father's training and spiritual study continued. My father reached mastership and was ordained by God on July 7, 1999 but he was still not yet Prophet, more was required. On October 22, 2012, twenty-five years since his full-time intensive training had begun, God ordained him as His chosen Prophet, and He has continued to raise him up further since. God works through my father in very direct and beneficial ways for his students. Hundreds and hundreds of students over the past thirty years have received God's eternal teachings through my father's instruction and mentoring. They have had personal experiences with the Divine which have transformed and greatly blessed their lives. My father's greatest joy is being used by God as a servant to share God's Ways and Truths with thirsty Souls and hungry seekers. In addition to mountain-top retreats, my father continues to spread God's ways and teachings that so greatly blessed his life and the lives of his loved ones in many ways.

The book you hold in your hand is but one of more than a dozen titles we have co-authored. These incredible testimonies of God's Love are being shared in print, eBook, audio, YouTube videos and podcasts in hopes of blessing others.

Maybe you are at a turning point in your life and looking for direction. Maybe you have a knowing there is more to life but not sure what that might be or how to find it. Or, maybe you are simply drawn to what you read and hear in our stories. God speaks to our hearts and calls each of us in many different ways. Like my father's journey demonstrates, it doesn't matter where you started or the twists, turns, or seeming dead-ends your life has taken; God wants us to know Him more fully, and for us to know our purpose within His creation. He wants us to experience His Love regardless of our religious path or lack there of. He always has a living Prophet here on earth to help us accomplish His desire for us – to show us the way home to Him and to experience more abundance in our life while we are still living here on earth. God's Prophet today is my father, Del Hall III. You have the opportunity to grow spiritually through God's teachings which Prophet shares. His guidance for a better life is available for you – please accept it.

Written by Del Hall IV

My Son, Del Hall IV

My son, Del Hall IV, joined Guidance for a Better Life as an instructor after fifteen years of in-class training with me, his father. He helped develop the five step "Keys to Spiritual Freedom" study program and facilitates the first two courses in the

Del Hall IV

program: Step One "Tools for Divine Guidance" and Step Two "Understanding Divine Guidance." Del also teaches people about the rich history of dream study and how to better recall their own dreams during the "Dream Study Workshops," which he hosts around the country. He is qualified to step-in and facilitate any of my retreats should the need arise.

Del is also Vice President of Marketing and helps with everything required to get the "good news" from Guidance for a Better Life out to hungry seekers: everything from book publishing, blogging, podcasts, and other social media outlets. He is co-author and book cover designer for many of our, thus far, fourteen published books.

My son loves the opportunity to work on creative projects for Guidance for a Better Life. From a very early age he has been an artist and loved creating artwork in multiple mediums. He was accepted into gifted art programs in Virginia Beach and then after high school graduation he attended the School of the Museum of Fine Arts in Boston. He is now a nationally exhibited artist and his paintings of the Light and Sound of God are in over seventy-five public and private collections. One of the greatest joys of the painting process for Del is using his paintings as an opportunity to share with others the inspiration behind them, God's Love and his experiences with the Light and Sound of God, the Holy Spirit, in contemplation and in waking life.

Del lives on the retreat center property in the Blue Ridge Mountains of Virginia with his wife and my three grandchildren whom they homeschool. He loves woodworking, tending to his vegetable garden, pruning his fruit trees, and helping maintain the beautiful three-hundred acres of retreat center property for students to enjoy. There is always something that needs attention on the land and Del is always up to the challenge. He loves to travel and spends his free time enjoying this beautiful country with his family in their RV.

My son has had multiple brain surgeries starting when he was seventeen years old for a recurring brain tumor. He credits God for surviving and thriving all this time when most with his condition do not. He looks to the sunrise everyday with gratitude for yet another chance at life. With that chance he desires to help me share the love and teachings of God that have so blessed our lives. I pray to God daily thanking Him for my son's good health.

Written by Prophet Del Hall III

What is the Role of God's Prophet?

An introductory understanding of God's handpicked and Divinely trained Prophet is necessary to fully benefit from reading this book. God ALWAYS has a living Prophet of His choice on Earth. He has a physical body with a limited number of students, but the inner spiritual side of Prophet is limitless. Spiritually he can help countless numbers of Souls all over the world, no matter what religion or path they are on — even if that is no path at all. He teaches the ways of God and shares the Light and Sound of God. He delivers the living Word of God. Prophet can teach you physically as well as through dreams, and he can lift you into the Heavens of God. He offers protection, peace, teachings, guidance, healing, and love.

Each of God's Prophets throughout history has a unique mission. One may only have a few students with the sole intent to keep God's teachings and truth alive. God may use another to change the course of history. God's Prophets are usually trained by both the current and former Prophets. The Prophet is tested and trained over a very long period of time. The earlier Prophets are physically gone but teach the new Prophet in the inner spiritual worlds. This serves two main purposes: the trainee becomes very adept at spiritual travel and gains wisdom from those in whose shoes he will someday walk. This is vital training because the Prophet is the one who must safely prepare and then take his students into the Heavens and back.

There are many levels of Heaven, also called planes or mansions. Saint Paul once claimed to know a man who went to the third Heaven. Actually it was Paul himself that went, but the pearl is, if there is a third Heaven, it presumes a first and second Heaven also exist. The first Heaven is often referred to as the Astral plane. Even on just that one plane of existence there are over one hundred sub-planes. This Heaven is where most people go after passing, unless they receive training while still here in their physical body. Without a guide who is trained properly in the ways of God a student could misunderstand the intended lesson and become confused as to what is truth. The inner worlds are enormous compared to the physical worlds. They are very real and can be explored safely when guided by God's Prophet.

Part of my mission is to share more of what is spiritually possible for you as a child of God. Few Souls know or understand that God's Prophet can safely guide God's children, while still alive physically, to their Heavenly Home. Taking a child of God into the Heavens is not the job of clergy. Clergy have a responsibility to pass on the teaching of their religion exactly as they were taught, not to add additional concepts or possibilities. If every clergy member taught their own personal belief system no religion could survive for long. Then the beautiful teachings of an earlier Prophet of God would be lost. Clergy can be creative in finding interesting and uplifting ways to share their teachings, but their job is to keep their religion intact. However, God sends His Prophets to build on the teachings of His past Prophets, to share God's Light and Love, to teach His language, and to guide Souls to their Heavenly Home.

There is ALWAYS MORE when it comes to God's teachings and truth. No one Prophet can teach ALL of God's ways. It may be that the audience of a particular time in history cannot absorb more wisdom. It could be due to a Prophet's limited time to teach and limited time in a physical body on Earth. Ultimately, it is that there is ALWAYS MORE! Each of God's Prophets brings additional teachings and opportunities for ways to draw closer to God, building on the work and teachings of former Prophets. That is one reason why Prophets of the past ask God to send another; to comfort, teach, and continue to help God's children grow into greater abundance. Former Prophets continue to have great love for God's children and want to see them continue to grow in accepting more of God's Love. One never needs to stop loving or accepting help from a past Prophet in order to grow with the help of the current Prophet. All true Prophets of God work together and help one another to do God's work.

All the testimonies in this book were written by students at the Guidance for a Better Life retreat center. It is here that the nature of God, the Holy Spirit, and the nature of Soul are EXPERIENCED under the guidance of a true living Prophet of God. Guidance for a Better Life is NOT a religion, it is a retreat center. God and His Prophet are NOT disparaging of any religion of love. However, the more a path defines itself with its teachings, dogma, or tenets, the more "walls" it inadvertently creates between the seeker and God. Sometimes it even puts God into a smaller box. God does not fit in any box. Prophet is for all Souls and is purposely not officially aligned with any path, but shows respect to all.

YOU can truly have an ABUNDANT LIFE through a personal and loving relationship with God, the Holy Spirit, and God's ordained Prophet. This is my primary message to you. Having a closer relationship with the Divine requires understanding the "Language of the Divine." God expresses His Love to us, His children, in many different and sometimes very subtle ways. Often His Love goes unrecognized and unaccepted because His language is not well known. The testimonies in this book have shown you some of the ways in which God expresses His Love. It is my hope that in reading this book, you have begun to learn more of the "Language of the Divine." The stories spanned from very subtle Divine guidance to profound examples of experiencing God up close and very personal. After reading this book I hope you now know your relationship with God has the potential to be more profound, more personal, and more loving than any organized religion on Earth currently teaches.

If you wish to develop a relationship with God's Prophet, seek the inner side of Prophet, for he is spiritually already with you. Few are able to meet the current physical incarnation and most people do not need to meet Prophet physically. Gently sing HU for a few minutes and then sing "Prophet" with love in your heart and he will respond. It may take time to recognize his presence, but it will come. The Light and Love that flows through him is the same that has flowed through all of God's true Prophets.

A more abundant life awaits you,

Prophet Del Hall III

Articles of Faith

Written by Prophet Del Hall III

1. We believe in one true God that is still living and active in our lives. He is knowable and wants a relationship with each of His children. He is the same God Jesus called FATHER, and is known by many names, including Heavenly Father. God wants a loving personal relationship with each of us, NOT one based upon fear or guilt.

2. The Holy Spirit is God's expression in all the worlds. It is in two parts, the Light and the Sound. It is through His Holy Spirit God communicates and delivers all His gifts: peace, clarity, love, joy, healings, correction, guidance, wisdom, comfort, truth, dreams, new revelations, and more.

3. God always has a chosen living Prophet to teach His ways, speak His living word, lift up Souls, and bring us closer to God. God's living Prophet is a concentrated aspect of the Holy Spirit, the Light and Sound, and is raised up and ordained by God directly. His Prophet is empowered and authorized to share God's Light

and Sound and to correct misunderstandings of His ways. There are two aspects of God's Prophet, an inner spiritual and outer physical Prophet. The inner Prophet can teach us through dreams, intuition, spiritual travel, inner communication, and his presence. The outer Prophet also teaches through his discourses, written word, and his presence. Prophet is always with us spiritually on the inner. Prophet points to and glorifies the Father.

4. God so loves the world and His children He has always had a long unbroken line of His chosen Prophets. They existed before Jesus and after Jesus. Jesus was God's Prophet and His actual SON. God's chosen Prophets are considered to be in the "role of God's Son," though NOT literally His Son. Only Jesus was literally His son. Prophets were sometimes called Paraclete. The Bible uses the word Comforter, but the original Greek word was Paraclete, which is more accurate. Paraclete implied an actual physical person who helps, counsels, encourages, advocates, comforts, and sets free.

5. Our real and eternal self is called Soul. We are Soul; we do NOT "have" a Soul. As Soul we are literally an individualized piece of God's Holy Spirit, thereby Divine in nature. We are made of

God's Light and Sound, which is actually God's Love. As an individual and uniquely experienced Soul you have free will, intelligence, imagination, opinions, clear and continuous access to Divine guidance, and immortality. As Soul we have an innate and profound spiritual growth potential. Soul has the ability to travel the Heavens spiritually with Prophet to gain truth and wisdom, and grow in love. Soul exists because God loves it.

6. We believe Soul equals Soul, in that God loves all Souls equally and each Soul has the same innate qualities and potential. Soul is neither male nor female, any particular race, nationality, or age. All Souls are children of God.

7. We believe in one eternal life as Soul. However, we believe Soul needs to incarnate many times into a physical body to learn and grow spiritually mature. Soul's journey home to God encompasses many lifetimes. A loving God does not expect His children to learn His ways in a single lifetime.

8. We believe Soul incarnates on Earth to grow in the ability to give and receive love.

9. We believe God is more interested in two Souls experiencing love for one another than in

their sexual preference.

10. It is God's will that a negative power exists to help Soul grow spiritually through challenges and hardships, thereby strengthening and maturing Soul. We are never given a challenge greater than our ability to find a solution. Soul has the ability to rise above any obstacles with God's help.

11. We study the Bible as an authentic teaching tool of God's ways, in addition to books and discourses authored by a Prophet chosen by God. We know the original Biblical writings have been altered in some cases by incorrect translations and political interference throughout the ages. God loves each of us regardless of our errors. We do not believe in God's eternal abandonment or damnation. He would never turn His back to us for eternity.

12. Karma is the way in which the Divine accounts for our actions, words, thoughts, and attitudes. One can create positive or negative karma. Karma is a blessing used to teach us responsibility. We do not have to earn God's Love, He loves us unconditionally.

13. We do not believe that a child is born in sin, though the child may have karma from a former

life. Karma, God's accounting system, explains our birth circumstances better than the concept of sin.

14. We believe that a living Prophet, including Jesus, can remove karma and sin when necessary to help us get started or to grow on the path to God. However, it is primarily our responsibility to live and grow in the ways of God, thereby not creating negative karma and sin.

15. There are four commandments of God in which we abide; First – Love God with all your heart, mind and soul; Second – Love your neighbor as yourself. We believe the Third is; "Seek ye first the Kingdom of God, and His righteousness." We believe this means that it is primarily our responsibility to draw close to God, learn His ways, and strive to live the way God would like us to live. God's Prophets are sent to show His ways. We believe our purpose, the Fourth Commandment, is to become spiritually mature to be used by God to bless His children. Becoming a co-worker with God is our primary purpose in life and the most rewarding attainment of Soul.

16. We believe all Souls upon translation, death of the physical body, go to the higher worlds, called Heavens, Planes, or Mansions, regardless

of their beliefs. The way they live life on Earth and the effort made to draw close to God impacts the area of Heaven they are to be sent. Those who draw close to a Prophet of God receive special care. We know of twelve distinct Heavens, not one. The primary abode of the Heavenly Father is in the twelfth Heaven, known as the "Ocean of Love and Mercy." We can visit God while we still live on Earth, but only if taken by His chosen Prophet and only as Soul, not in a physical body.

17. We believe prayer is communication with God and is an extreme privilege. God hears every prayer from the heart whether or not we recognize a response. Singing an ancient name of God, HU, is our foundational prayer. It expresses love and gratitude to God and is unencumbered by words. Singing HU has the potential to raise us up in consciousness making us more receptive to God's Love, Light, and guiding Hand. After praying it is best to spend time listening to God. Prayer should never be rote or routine. We desire to trust God and surrender to His Will rather than our own will.

18. We believe it is our responsibility to stay spiritually nourished. When Soul is nourished and fortified it becomes activated and we are more

receptive and have clearer communication with the Divine. We believe when Jesus said "give us this day our daily bread," he meant daily spiritual nourishment, not physical bread. This can be done by singing HU, reading scripture, praying, dream study, demonstrating gratitude for our blessings, being in a living Prophet's physical presence, or in his inner presence, or listening to his words.

19. We believe TRUTH has the power to improve every area of our lives, but only if understood, accepted, and integrated into our lives.

20. We believe God and His Prophet guide us in our sleeping dreams and awake dreams as a gift of love. God's Prophet teaches how to understand both types of dreams. All areas of our lives may be blessed by the wisdom God offers each of us directly in dreams.

21. Gratitude is extremely important on our path of love. It is literally the secret of love. Developing an attitude of gratitude is necessary to becoming spiritually mature. Recognizing and being grateful for the blessings of God in our lives is vital to building a loving and trusting relationship with God and His chosen Prophet. A relationship with God's Prophet is THE KEY to everything good and a

life more abundant.

22. We believe in being good stewards of our blessings. We recognize them as gifts of love from God and make the effort to have remembrance. Remembering our blessings helps to keep our heart open to God and builds trust in God's Love for us.

23. We believe in giving others the freedom to make their own choices and live their lives as they wish. We expect the same in return.

24. We believe the Love and Blessings of God and His Prophet are available to all who are receptive. If one desires guidance and help from Prophet, ask from the heart and sing "Prophet." He will respond. One does not need to meet Prophet physically to receive help. To be taught by Prophet it is best to attend a retreat with him in the physical. However, much can be gained by reading or listening to his teachings.

25. We have a responsibility to do our part and let God and His Prophet do their part. This responsibility brings freedom. Our goal is to remain spiritually nourished, live in balance and harmony, and serve God as a co-worker. Anything is possible with God if we do our part. We pray to use our God given free will in a way

that our actions, thoughts, words, and attitudes testify and bear witness to the Glory and Love of God.

26. We believe there is always more to learn and grow in God's ways and truth. One cannot remain the same spiritually. One must make the effort to move forward or risk falling backward. To grow in consciousness requires change. Spiritual wisdom gained during our earthly incarnations can be taken to the other worlds when we translate, and into future lifetimes, unlike our physical possessions.

Contact Information

Guidance for a Better Life is a worldwide mentoring program provided by Prophet Del Hall III and his son Del Hall IV. Personal one-on-one mentoring at our retreat center is our premier offering and the most direct and effective way to grow spiritually. Spiritual tools, guided exercises, and in-depth discourses on the eternal teachings of God are provided to help one become more aware of and receptive to His Holy Spirit and the abundance that awaits. With this personally-tailored guidance one begins to more fully recognize God's Love daily in their lives, both the dramatic and the very subtle. Over time our mentoring reduces fear, worry, anxiety, lack of purpose, feelings of unworthiness, guilt, and confusion; replacing those negative aspects of life with an abundance of peace, clarity, joy, wisdom, love, and self-respect leading to a more personal relationship with God, more than most know is possible. We also offer our dozen books, YouTube videos, and podcast.

Guidance for a Better Life
P.O. Box 219
Lyndhurst, Virginia 22952
(540) 377-6068
contact@guidanceforabetterlife.com
www.guidanceforabetterlife.com

"A Growing Testament to the Power of God's Love One Profound Book at a Time."

SPECIALIZED TOPICS

Whether you wish to reconnect with a loved one who has passed, understand how you too can experience God's Light, improve your marriage, or learn how to understand your dreams, these incredible books have you covered.

TESTIMONIES OF GOD'S LOVE SERIES

God expresses His Love every day in many different and sometimes subtle ways. Often this love goes unrecognized because the ways in which God communicates are not well known. Each of the books in this series contains fifty true stories that will help you learn to better recognize the Love of God in your life.

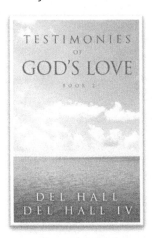
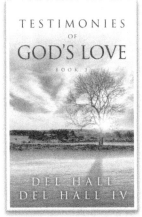
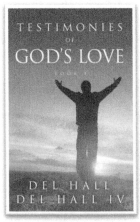
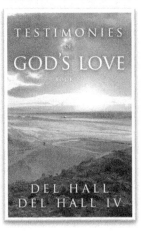

JOURNEY TO A TRUE SELF-IMAGE SERIES

This series includes intimate and unique stories that many readers will be able to personally identify with, enjoy, and learn from. They will help the reader transcend the false images people often carry about themselves - first and foremost that they are only their physical mind and body. The authors share their journeys of recognizing and coming to more fully accept their true self-image, that of Soul – an eternal child of God.

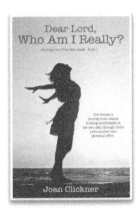

Made in the USA
Middletown, DE
16 August 2021